T·R·A·D·E
POLICY
AND
U.S.
COMPETITIVENESS

T·R·A·D·E
POLICY
AND
U.S.
COMPETITIVENESS

EDITED BY
CLAUDE E. BARFIELD
AND
JOHN H. MAKIN

American Enterprise Institute for Public Policy Research
Washington, D.C.

Claude E. Barfield is a resident fellow in science and technology policy and director of the Competing in a Changing World Economy project at AEI. John H. Makin is a resident scholar and director of Fiscal Policy Studies at AEI.

Distributed by arrangement with

UPA, Inc.
4720 Boston Way
Lanham, Md. 20706
3 Henrietta Street
London WC2E 8LU England

Library of Congress Cataloging-in-Publication Data

Trade policy and U.S. competitiveness.

   (AEI studies ; 461)

1. United States—Commercial policy.
2. Competition—United States.   3. Competition,
International.   I. Barfield, Claude E.
II. Makin, John H.   III. Series.
HF1455.T65   1987   382'.3'0973   87–18831
ISBN 0-8447-3633-3 (alk. paper)
ISBN 0-8447-3634-1 (pbk. : alk. paper)
AEI Studies 461

1 3 5 7 9 10 8 6 4 2

Printed in the United States of America

Contents

PARTICIPANTS   xi

PREFACE   xv

PART ONE
RENEWING AMERICA'S COMPETITIVENESS

1 RENEWING AMERICA'S COMPETITIVENESS
James A. Baker III   3

    Removing International Barriers to Trade 5
    Removing Domestic Barriers to Growth 6
    The Cultural Roots of Competitiveness 6
    Conclusion 7

PART TWO
LEADERSHIP IN TRADE POLICY

2 CONGRESS AND THE PRESIDENT—THE ISSUES
Alan F. Holmer   13

3 TRANSFERRING AUTHORITY TO THE TRADE
REPRESENTATIVE *Kent Hughes*   17

4 THE CONGRESSIONAL PERSPECTIVE *Joanna Shelton*   19

5 TRADE POLICY AND THE TRADE REPRESENTATIVE
William D. Eberle   22

PART THREE
WHAT THE NUMBERS SAY:
SUMMARY OF THE COMPETITIVE POSITION OF THE UNITED STATES

6 OVERVIEW OF THE U.S. COMPETITIVE POSITION TODAY
Allen J. Lenz   27

PART FOUR
THE DETERMINANTS OF COMPETITIVENESS

7 THE ROLE OF DOMESTIC POLICY IN ADDRESSING TRADE
PROBLEMS   *Sven W. Arndt*   39

8 THE COMPETITIVENESS GAP   *Gary C. Hufbauer*   43

9 SUCCESSFUL EXPORTING: WHAT THE PRIVATE SECTOR
CAN DO   *William Lilley III*   46

PART FIVE
TRADE LEGISLATION, TRADE POLICY, AND U.S. COMPETITIVENESS

10 ISSUES AFFECTING THE FORMULATION OF A TRADE BILL
C. Michael Aho   53

11 TRADE POLICY: A DEMOCRAT'S VIEW
Robert T. Matsui   55

12 THE NEED AND THE PROSPECTS FOR A TRADE BILL IN 1987
Sander M. Levin   58

13 TRADE POLICY: A REPUBLICAN'S VIEW   *Tom DeLay*   61

14 COMPETITIVENESS AND TRADE POLICY: A VIEW FROM THE
ADMINISTRATION   *David A. Walters*   65

15 TRADE LEGISLATION: A VIEW FROM THE EUROPEAN
COMMUNITY   *Sir Roy Denman*   70

16 TRADE POLICY: A VIEW FROM JAPAN   *Ryozo Hayashi*   73

PART SIX
INDUSTRIAL ADJUSTMENT: INDUSTRIAL POLICY REVIVED?

17 REFORM OF SECTION 201 IMPORT RELIEF   *Don J. Pease*   77

18 PROTECTIONISM   *Daniel Oliver*   81

19 THE IMPORTANCE OF PROCESS   *Alan Wolff*   86

20 MAKING RELIEF CONDITIONAL ON ADJUSTMENT
Paul C. Rosenthal   90

21 THE POLITICS OF INDUSTRIAL ADJUSTMENT
Claude E. Barfield, Daniel Oliver, and Don J. Pease   92

PART SEVEN
LABOR ADJUSTMENT:
AID OR BARRIER TO COMPETITIVENESS?

22 MORE OPTIONS FOR THE DISPLACED WORKER
Malcolm R. Lovell, Jr.   97

23 THE URGENCY OF ASSISTANCE TO DISPLACED WORKERS
Jay Rockefeller   100

24 MYTHS SURROUNDING DISPLACED WORKERS
Howard D. Samuel   104

25 LABOR ADJUSTMENT, RETRAINING, AND ADVANCE NOTICE
OF CLOSINGS *Marvin H. Kosters*   107

26 BALANCING COMPETITIVENESS WITH ASSISTANCE TO WORKERS
*Marvin L. Esch, Marvin H. Kosters, Malcolm R. Lovell, Jr.,
Jay Rockefeller, and Howard D. Samuel*   109

PART EIGHT
COMPETITIVENESS: A MAJOR CAMPAIGN ISSUE IN '88?

27 IS COMPETITIVENESS A GENUINE ISSUE?
Norman Ornstein   117

28 A DEMOCRAT'S VIEW *Paul G. Kirk, Jr.*   119

29 A REPUBLICAN'S VIEW *Edward J. Rollins*   122

30 WHAT THE POLLS TELL US *Karlyn H. Keene*   127

31 THE MEANING OF COMPETITIVENESS *Karlyn H. Keene,
Paul G. Kirk, Jr., Norman Ornstein, Edward J. Rollins,
and John H. Makin*   131

GLOSSARY OF INTERNATIONAL TRADE TERMS   137

Participants

C. *Michael Aho*
Senior Fellow in Economics
Council on Foreign Relations

Sven W. Arndt
Professor of Economics
University of California, Santa Cruz

James A. Baker III
Secretary of the Treasury
U.S. Department of the Treasury

Claude E. Barfield
Resident Fellow and
Director of Science and Technology Policy Studies
American Enterprise Institute

Tom DeLay
Republican Member from Texas
U.S. House of Representatives

Sir Roy Denman
Head of Delegation to the United States
Commission of the European Communities

William D. Eberle
President
Manchester Associates

Marvin L. Esch
Director of Seminars and Programs
American Enterprise Institute

Ryozo Hayashi
Representative
Japanese Ministry of International Trade and Industry

Alan F. Holmer
General Counsel
Office of the U.S. Trade Representative

Gary C. Hufbauer
Marcus Wallenberg Professor of International Financial Diplomacy
School of Foreign Service
Georgetown University

Kent Hughes
Staff Director
House Foreign Affairs Subcommittee on
International Policy and Trade

Karlyn H. Keene
Resident Fellow and Managing Editor of *Public Opinion*
American Enterprise Institute

Paul G. Kirk, Jr.
Chairman
Democratic National Committee

Marvin H. Kosters
Resident Scholar and Director of Economic Policy Studies
American Enterprise Institute

Allen J. Lenz
Director
Office of Trade and Investment Analysis of
the International Trade Administration
U.S. Department of Commerce

Sander M. Levin
Democratic Member from Michigan
U.S. House of Representatives

William Lilley III
President
American Business Conference

Malcolm R. Lovell, Jr.
Distinguished Visiting Professor and Executive-in-Residence
School of Government and Business Administration
George Washington University

John H. Makin
Resident Scholar and Director of Fiscal Policy Studies
American Enterprise Institute

Robert T. Matsui
Democratic Member from California
U.S. House of Representatives

Daniel Oliver
Chairman
Federal Trade Commission

Norman Ornstein
Resident Scholar
American Enterprise Institute

Don J. Pease
Democratic Member from Ohio
U.S. House of Representatives

Jay Rockefeller
Democratic Member from West Virginia
U.S. Senate

Edward J. Rollins
Managing Partner
Russo, Watts, Rollins & Reilly

Paul C. Rosenthal
Partner
Collier, Shannon, Rill & Scott

Howard D. Samuel
Cochair, OSHA/Environmental Network
Member, Presidential Commission on Industrial Competitiveness

Joanna Shelton
Professional Staff Member
House Ways and Means Subcommittee on Trade

David A. Walters
Chief Economist
Office of the U.S. Trade Representative

Alan Wolff
Senior Partner
Dewey, Ballantine, Bushby, Palmer & Wood

Preface

Economists and trade policy experts have offered a bewildering variety of explanations for America's trade deficits and competitive difficulties in world markets in the mid to late 1980s. The president made "competitiveness" a major theme in his 1987 State of the Union Address and, having submitted a set of initiatives to fulfill his goals, embarked on a nationwide campaign during the spring to sell his program. Meanwhile, a quite different analysis and a quite different set of proposed solutions emerged from the two houses of Congress.

In late April 1987, after the major policy proposals were on the table but before significant decisions had been made, AEI convened a conference to evaluate the likely results of the policy prescriptions advocated by the president, members of Congress, and numerous private interest groups. We brought to the conference table high administration officials, including the secretary of the Treasury and the chairman of the Federal Trade Commission; leading congressional spokesmen for the sharply different legislative approaches under consideration; and trade policy experts and representatives of the private sector.

The major issues dealt with included:

- the central factors controlling U.S. competitiveness
- the role of the president and Congress in the formulation and implementation of trade policy
- the implications and likely consequences of the import restrictions Congress is considering
- the public and private role and responsibility for industrial and labor adjustment
- the issue of competitiveness and the 1988 presidential election

The result was a series of lively discussions on the issues surrounding U.S. trade policy and the determinants of U.S. competitiveness. In view of the consistently high level of cogent information and perspective put forward at the conference, AEI moved with dispatch to publish the proceedings while the White House and Congress attempted to come to final decisions on trade legislation.

The issues discussed here will continue to confront the world economy, and, appropriately, the discussions at the conference went far beyond a proximate focus on possible trade legislation in 1987. We think that, regardless of their position on individual issues, policy makers and members of Congress will find in this volume clear and valid arguments on the major questions posed by trade legislation and by the enduring issue of U.S. competitiveness.

CLAUDE E. BARFIELD
JOHN H. MAKIN

Part One

Renewing America's Competitiveness

1

Renewing America's Competitiveness

James A. Baker III

Competitiveness now competes with balanced budgets and compassion as this town's most popular phrase. Everybody supports competitiveness, but too often the specific policies endorsed in its name actually make us less competitive. It's not unlike the line in the country and western song I once heard: "Calling it love is no excuse for what we're doing."

How do we measure the competitiveness of an economy or a society? It seems clear enough that a competitive economy is not simply an economy that has a trade surplus—by that standard Brazil is better off than the United States. By that standard, too, Japan is better off than we are. Yet the United States has created 13 million new jobs since 1982, while Japan has had only sluggish job growth.

Clearly, by competitiveness we have to mean something more, something broader than mere trade statistics. Perhaps we mean something like this: a competitive nation is a nation with a growing economy that is creating jobs and lifting incomes without inflation, and that is getting the most from its natural and human resources. In short, a competitive nation is one that has what most economists would call a healthy, vibrant economy.

By that standard, I have to admit, the United States could do a number of things better. Yet by that same standard the United States is already doing much better than in the late 1970s and much better than our critics like to admit. Let me cite a few indicators.

- Since 1982 America's real economic growth has averaged nearly 4 percent a year, the same rate as Japan and a much better performance than most of Europe. In the 1970s, Japan and most of Europe consistently outperformed the United States.
- This American growth, moreover, has sustained world growth. Without America's recovery—now into its fifty-third month—most of

the world, especially the export economies of Europe and Asia, would have grown only sluggishly, if at all.

• This growth is also more sustainable now than it was in the 1970s because today growth is noninflationary. Since 1981 the U.S. rate of inflation has averaged below 4 percent.

• We have also had impressive growth in personal income and assets, especially after taxes. Real per capita disposable income has grown by 2.6 percent a year since 1982, roughly twice the rate of the late 1970s and the best performance since the 1960s. And the stock market boom has added more than $1 trillion to investors' assets. The market, you may recall, was flat during virtually the entire last half of the 1970s.

• We are also more productive. Our productivity growth still trails that of our leading competitor, Japan, but the difference is now smaller than it was in the late 1970s. Our manufacturing productivity has risen at an average annual rate of 3.5 percent in the past six years, faster than at any time in the past three decades.

• Finally, we have had enormous competitive gains, in both service and efficiency, as a result of deregulation. Our airlines are now far more efficient than airlines elsewhere in the world, and our consumers are paying much lower fares.

I mention all this not to overlook our weaknesses but only to underscore that we have made progress. Clearly, we as a nation have things we can improve on, but we do ourselves a disservice if all we do is insist that the economy is going over the cliff.

Let me make two other general points about competitiveness. First, the economic rise of our allies and trading partners was to some extent inevitable and even desirable. Surely the free world is stronger today because Japan and Korea have tied themselves into the free trading system and have prospered as a result. Surely Europe's postwar recovery—what historian Paul Johnson calls "the European Lazarus"—presents us with benefits as well as challenges. We need to keep competition in perspective and to remember that trade is not a zero-sum game. You may recall the French best-seller of the 1960s, *The American Challenge*, whose thesis was that American multinationals were going to take over the world. Although many American companies have done well, so have French and German and Italian and Japanese companies.

Second, we also need to keep in mind that a competitive society is not something we can legislate from Washington. Government can surely do things to help but we are deceiving ourselves if we think that government can do it alone. Our efforts must be much broader and much deeper. They must reach into our schools, our communities, our companies, and even our families. Competitiveness—as much a cultural undertaking as an economic or a political one—requires changing minds as much as changing policies. To borrow a line from George Will, it requires as much soulcraft as statecraft.

Removing International Barriers to Trade

The federal government nonetheless has a role to play in promoting American competitiveness both at home and internationally. Overseas, I believe our principal duty—and the centerpiece of the Reagan administration trade policy—is to seek to remove foreign barriers to trade. We have done that aggressively—for example, through the very important multilateral forum of the GATT. In last fall's preparatory talks for the new Uruguay trade round, we succeeded in getting most of our priorities on the agenda. We will now be discussing for the first time in a GATT round trade in agriculture and services and the protection of intellectual property—all areas in which America is competitive.

We have also worked to remove barriers on a bilateral basis. Our initiative to create a free trade zone with Canada could be one of this administration's most important accomplishments. We have moved aggressively to remove barriers to American products in nations reluctant to change. Again, the result has been progress—on cigarettes and copyright laws in Korea, on tariffs and investment laws in Taiwan, and even in Japan, in financial markets and some consumer goods. All of these countries must continue to liberalize, for the sake of both the world trading system and their own standards of living, but their reluctance to move further is not the result of any lack of prodding.

Moreover, our international economic efforts do not focus only on trade barriers. We recognize that trade issues cannot be separated from other macroeconomic policy issues. The world economy today is one constantly flowing circle of capital and goods. Trade accounts catch and measure that flow at only one spot on the circle.

In the past two years I have tried to persuade our major industrial allies to work with us to coordinate our economic policies better. We have made some important progress. Substantial exchange rate adjustment has also been accomplished over the past two years, so that today we are better positioned to promote growth and to reduce external imbalances. In February we took another step forward with the Louvre Accord to promote faster world growth and to foster stability of exchange rates, and we have since renewed the Louvre

5

commitments. From conversations with Mr. Abe it is clear that Japan intends to take strong steps to stimulate its economy to meet its commitments under the Louvre Accord.

Let me emphasize that *all seven* major industrial nations remain fully committed to strengthening policy coordination, promoting growth, and cooperating to foster stability of exchange rates. We all believe a further decline of the dollar would be counterproductive to our efforts.

Removing Domestic Barriers to Growth

We cannot blame all our competitive problems on foreign policies or on trade barriers. We have often created our own barriers to growth, and government has been a major culprit. I have in mind such things as product liability judgments that have caused insurance rates to soar, counterproductive taxes, archaic antitrust laws that judge markets in national instead of global terms, and countless regulations that raise costs for industry.

For its part, Japan has often been wiser. We should appreciate that Japan usually does not tax capital gain and that, at least from the 1960s through the early 1980s, Japan had a total tax burden lower than that of any other major industrial country. In short, Japan's government often works with, not against, industry when it devises public policy.

We neither can nor should import all Japan's government habits. Indeed, the Japanese can learn from us in promoting enough domestic competition in consumer goods and services to keep prices low. But we should ask hard questions every time we propose some higher tax or some new regulation. Do higher taxes really make us more competitive? Do additional medical expenses required of employers make us more competitive, especially when we already spend more of our GNP on health care than Japan does? Do our barriers to interstate banking make us more competitive, when foreign banks do not operate under the same restrictions?

If our competitiveness debate does nothing else but force us to ask and to face up to these hard questions, it will clearly have been worthwhile.

The Cultural Roots of Competitiveness

Our effort should not stop with government—indeed, cannot depend on government—if we are to succeed. We must also examine our own culture. We must question our own complacency. Two areas in particular seem to require the greatest attention: education and our corporate culture.

Some of you may have seen the recent *Newsweek* article "A Dunce Cap for America." Some of you may have also seen the "60 Minutes" in which American college students said they thought Beirut was in Ireland and that Joseph McCarthy was a famous Communist. These are symptoms of educational weakness. They are signs of competitive weakness made in America.

For several years the quality of American education has been a front-burner issue. While American children spend 180 days each year in school, Japanese children spend 240 days. Indeed, American students do worse in mathematics than students of virtually any other industrial nation. And while spending on U.S. public education soared during the 1960s and 1970s, performance by any measure fell. If our comparative advantage in the future is really going to be our human capital, education must surely be one of our highest priorities.

It is also fair to ask whether our companies have done all they can to adapt to the era of global competition. Although many have done well around the world, some seem tied to old practices and domestic markets, in particular to old habits of labor confrontation rather than to what the Japanese call *kaizen*, the crusade for improvement that involves all employees in promoting a company's success. We all know how Japan has benefited from its pattern of generally cooperative labor-management relations. We must examine our own corporate habits as we pursue global markets.

Cooper Procter, the former president of Procter & Gamble, once put it this way: "The chief problem of big business today is to shape its policy so that each worker will feel that he is a vital part of his company, with a personal responsibility for its success and a chance to share in the successes." He said that nearly 100 years ago, at the time that his company introduced profit sharing.

Conclusion

I do not believe we can become more competitive by passing a protectionist trade bill. We can become competitive only by competing, not by closing ourselves off from the world. We live today, unalterably, in a new world of global markets and global competition. We cannot run and we cannot hide—except at great cost to ourselves and to our standard of living.

We cannot seek to import all of what the Japanese or Germans do best, but we can draw on the unique strengths of the American system to build a more competitive industry and society. We have our diversity that tolerates new ideas, our federalism that encourages political experiment, the genius of our immigrants drawn here by opportunity, our capacity for experiment and initiative—these can and should be the real roots of America's renewed competitiveness.

Thank you.

Discussion

QUESTION: Mr. Secretary, the Gephardt amendment is probably going to be on the floor next week. How active is the lobbying going to be from the White House? There is every indication that the amendment will pass the House. Senator Dole has said that something very like it will pass the Senate, offering, obviously, veto bait. What efforts are being made to stop it?

SECRETARY BAKER: Not just the White House but the entire administration is very active in opposition to that amendment. I think there will be a provision in the House rule that will permit a vote specifically on that amendment. There may also be a provision for an opposition substitute bill. Let me assure you that the administration intends to be active and vigorous in its opposition.

QUESTION: Mr. Baker, a lot of people are saying that the administration has not made a strong enough commitment to stop the decline of the dollar. With the decline of the yen, people are saying that it is time for the administration to demonstrate its commitment by reviving the yen bonds. Is this being considered in Treasury?

SECRETARY BAKER: That question was advanced quite some time ago. The matter has been considered. We are unlikely to undertake it now. There are arguments both in favor and against doing so, arguments that depend to some extent on one's interpretation of market psychology. It is our view that some people might well view that as a lack of confidence by the United States in its own currency. Therefore, we do not think it is appropriate.

QUESTION: On the question raised by Mr. Abe when he was here on the $30 billion development fund for Latin America, what is your initial response? I am sure Mr. Nakasone will discuss that. And what do you think about the ruling by parliament against Nakasone's attempts to be more conciliatory toward U.S. wishes?

SECRETARY BAKER: We do not have all the details of the steps that the government of Japan will take to fulfill the commitments it made in Paris in the Louvre Accord and reaffirmed here a couple of weeks ago. From our conversations with Mr. Abe when he was here, we are satisfied that Japan is moving to implement those commitments, but we are not in a position until the prime minister gets here to give you all the specifics. We were pleased to see the budget pass the Diet because a supplemental budget designed to stimulate domestic demand in Japan cannot be passed until the basic budget gets through the legislature.

QUESTION: Mr. Secretary, you spoke about the high priority that the administration is putting on the Canadian talks. What is the likelihood of getting a broad agreement before the congressional deadline this fall, and what would be the consequences of not completing those talks by the fall?

SECRETARY BAKER: We are under a deadline of something like September; so we must keep pushing forward if we expect to see a free trade agreement with Canada. If we are not ready by some time in September, we may not get there because of the authority that the administration has and must have from Congress to conduct these kinds of negotiations.

QUESTION: Mr. Secretary, what do you think of H.R. 3 without the Gephardt amendment as it currently stands?

SECRETARY BAKER: We have some problems with H.R. 3 quite apart from the Gephardt amendment. It is a collection of provisions from almost every committee in the House. Each committee was invited to throw its ideas into the pot, and some things in that pot would be very detrimental to America's becoming more competitive.

For instance, there is a provision requiring preclearance of investment in the United States. One of the strengths of the U.S. economy has been its openness to investment. We are the leaders in bringing that message to the rest of the world, to open their regimes for investment so that they can prosper from the free flow of capital; it would be devastating if we limited investment in the United States. There are many other objectionable provisions.

QUESTION: Mr. Secretary, the Farm Credit Administration is asking for financial aid today, saying an emergency situation exists. They face default. How much financial assistance from Treasury will you have to provide for them?

SECRETARY BAKER: Some legislation passed a year or so ago restructuring the Farm Credit Administration gave it the right to look to us for assistance during liquidity crunches. I am not in a position to tell you what the amount of that might be.

QUESTION: They will receive that, though, sir?

SECRETARY BAKER: I can't even tell you that. At the very earliest the request came in an hour or so ago. I need a chance to look at it.

QUESTION: Mr. Secretary, Ambassador Yeutter and Secretary Lyng were in Tokyo these past few days, I believe primarily about agricultural products. My impression is they are coming away empty-handed again. My question is, do you have any ideas for dealing with that?

SECRETARY BAKER: I mentioned that becoming competitive involves our doing a whole host of things, one of which is breaking down foreign barriers to U.S. products. We continue to be aggressive in doing that. President Reagan is the first president to self-initiate unfair trading cases, 301 cases, and we have self-initiated quite a number. Over the past two years we have been very aggressive in petitioning other countries to open their markets to our products and breaking down barriers and in asking them to increase their growth to the extent that they can consistently with maintaining the gains the world has made against inflation, so that we can harmonize our economic policies and see more growth worldwide.

QUESTION: Mr. Secretary, could you give us your reaction to the sharp rise in inflation reported this morning?

SECRETARY BAKER: You are probably referring to the four-tenths of 1 percent increase for March. That reflects primarily what we have been predicting for some time—an increase in oil prices. In 1986, this country enjoyed the lowest inflation rate in over twenty-five years, 1.1 percent, but we have been saying for some time we would be unlikely to maintain that. In fact, we have forecast a higher rate for 1987, and the statistics that were released are consistent with our forecast.

Part Two

Leadership in Trade Policy

2

Congress and the President— the Issues

Alan F. Holmer

In the executive branch and Congress right now, there is no more timely topic than competitiveness and U.S. trade policy. In the trade area, Congress has a special relationship with the president in view of its power in Article I of the Constitution to regulate foreign commerce and the president's implied Article II powers with respect to foreign affairs. Since international trade perches at the nexus between the two, a closer consultative relationship has developed between Congress and the executive branch in this area.

Historically, Congress took a much more aggressive role with respect to trade policy until 1930. It legislated tariff increases and tariff reductions. The term "nontariff barriers" had not even been coined. But the debacle over the Smoot-Hawley Tariff Act of 1930 and its contribution to the Depression encouraged Congress to cede a greater role to the executive branch and to the president in this increasingly complex area. Initially the president was given a series of three-year delegations to reduce tariffs in exchange for reciprocal tariff cuts by our trading partners. Since the start of this reciprocal trade agreements program in 1934, Congress has incrementally insisted on more and more complicated safeguards to ensure that the president take congressional concerns into account in his decisions.

This trend has been exacerbated by the increased importance of nontariff barriers, since the scope and range of actions that could be taken by the president are difficult for Congress to anticipate. For example, in the Trade Agreements Act of 1979, Congress effectively established five such safeguards. It established increased judicial review of the dumping and countervailing duty laws. It established the legislative veto that has since been modified after the court's Chaddha decision. It required consultation and reporting requirements. It required a specific sunset, usually of five years, and required that

13

Congress specify in statute what the U.S. government's negotiating objectives were in trade negotiations.

I would like to analyze a few specific issues—presidential negotiating authority in the Uruguay Round; section 201, the fair trade statute in our trade laws, which is intended to provide temporary relief for a U.S. industry facing increased imports; and section 301 of our trade laws, the principal statute used to pry open foreign markets to U.S. exports. In those three crucial areas—negotiating authority and sections 301 and 201—the administration is reasonably satisfied with what has come out of the House process. With respect to legislation pending before the Senate Finance Committee, that is not the case.

In regard to negotiating authority, every trade bill in the past two decades has had the same formula. Sue Schwab, in Senator Danforth's office, says that the formula is X minus Y plus Z. X is whatever the administration wants; Y is whatever restrictions Congress places on what the administration wants; and Z is what Congress forces the administration to eat in order to get X minus Y. The question we have to ask ourselves as we address the Senate bill is, Where's the X? What is so important in that piece of legislation to the administration? What gives the administration any incentive to sign that legislation into law?

The Senate bill grants the president the authority that he already has under the Constitution to negotiate with foreign governments. The key issue is the so-called fast track—that is, once the president or his trade representative initials a trade agreement, what is the process that will be followed to implement the agreement in domestic law?

In the 1974 act and the 1979 act, Congress established the so-called fast track that allows the administration, once it has reached an agreement, to bring the implementing domestic legislation to Congress for an up or down vote without amendment. That is much more important in the Senate than in the House, because the senators give up their right to filibuster and to offer amendments on the Senate floor. In the House, that procedure is not nearly as prevalent.

S. 490 says that the administration has the right to submit to Congress a detailed trade policy statement and that Congress will then consider on a fast track whether or not it will grant access to congressional fast track procedures. Essentially, it is a fast track built on a fast track.

From the administration's perspective, we went through an agonizing process in the House, and we are now going through one in the Senate Finance Committee. The committee is indicating to us in great detail the negotiating objectives for the United States in the Uruguay Round and the overall U.S. trade policy as reflected in that legislation. As part of that process, it seems to us, the administration should be given access to the fast track.

In regard to section 201, we keep hearing from Congress—though less from the House than from the Senate—of a need for increased certainty and increased predictability (read increased import relief) under section 201.

What has caused members of the Senate and some in the House to conclude that this administration has blue-penciled section 201 out of the statute books? Although we have read that in editorials and elsewhere, nothing could be further from the truth. There have been sixteen section 201 cases filed during this administration. Ten times, the International Trade Commission provided no relief. In six cases, the ITC found injury and asked the president to provide import relief.

In four of those six cases, the president provided relief, far more meaningful relief than many in this room, I'm sure, would think appropriate: for the specialty steel industry, for the carbon steel industry, for the motorcycle industry, and for the wood shakes and shingles industry. Only two times in more than six years has the president said no to relief under section 201. In the copper case, we found that the number of copper fabricators' jobs that would have been placed at risk was six times the number of copper miners' jobs that would have been saved. In the footwear case, despite tremendous political pressure, the president concluded that providing footwear relief would result in about $3 billion in retaliation against U.S. exports and about $3 billion in increased consumer costs and that the import relief would make no difference as to what parts of the footwear industry lived or died.

We believe that is an impeccable record, and we see no reason whatsoever for a change to be made in presidential discretion under section 201.

Section 301 is a bit more complicated. Again, there is a desire for more predictability, but the tone is more troublesome. It reflects a loss of faith, particularly by members of the Senate, in negotiated settlements to trade problems and in our current agreements. There is a sense that negotiating an agreement will just let the other country off scot free.

In testimony before the Senate Finance Committee, Ambassador Yeutter and I have raised what ought to be the key question about presidential authority in section 301: Does this amendment help or hurt the ability of U.S. negotiators to pry open foreign markets to U.S.

exports? If we say in every instance that, unless we achieve a negotiated solution by a certain date, we will retaliate, we will not be successful.

One last point: It is imperative, as Congress writes the 1987 trade bill, that we do it with an eye to the future. The United States will not always have a $170 billion trade deficit. In fact, if you believe many of the economists, we will have to have a substantial trade surplus in the 1990s to pay our enormous foreign debt.

I can imagine how I would feel if a foreign trade official called me into his office, stuck a mandatory retaliation gun to my head, and said, "We in Country X have unilaterally decided that U.S. trade practices are unfair, and we want you to get rid of your steel quotas and your textile quotas and your machine tool quotas and your sugar quotas and your meat quotas and your peanut quotas and your cotton quotas and your quotas on dairy products and your buy-America provisions and your section 337 and your agricultural export subsidies and your price support programs. We think the way you administer your dumping and countervailing duty law is inconsistent with the GATT and the Subsidies Code and the Dumping Code. Get rid of your fishing laws and your custom user fees and your semiconductor third-country dumping agreement. We unilaterally consider all of them unfair. Get rid of all of them, and do it in fifteen months—six months if you enact the Gephardt amendment. Do it in the glare of the public spotlight. And if you don't, we're going to whack you."

My point is not to justify foreign unfair trade practices by highlighting our own, but that trade-distorted practices are in place in the United States and elsewhere in the world because of very powerful domestic political pressures. And it is impossible for anyone, even the U.S. trade representative or the Senate Finance Committee or the Ways and Means Committee, to wave away those practices with a magic wand that we call section 301.

3

Transferring Authority to the Trade Representative

Kent Hughes

I was asked particularly to comment on why there is an apparent trend toward limiting presidential discretion and shifting authority to the U.S. trade representative. Even where the law allows presidential actions, there is a sense of frustration that action has not been taken and an attempt to legislate that action. What lies behind this?

As Alan Holmer mentioned, there is, in fact, a constitutional responsibility for foreign economic policy that lies with the Congress. But it has, as Alan suggested, been exercised in very different ways. The hearings that accompanied the Smoot-Hawley Tariff Act show that everyone under the sun wanted a specific kind of tariff relief. After that experience, a considerable amount of authority was delegated to the executive branch.

Since World War II, that tide has gradually been reversed. Part of the reversal, of course, is related to tactical considerations and whatever the current trade deficit happens to be. Sometimes a proposal indicates nothing more than a desire to urge the executive branch to act. That was part of the impetus behind the original Rostenkowski-Bentsen-Gephardt proposal. It was targeted at the executive branch as well as at Japan. It helped open the doors to a pragmatic wing that suggested action on the dollar and other issues.

In addition to that, however, some long-term trends are at work. Since the 1960s, Congress has shown a desire to move the trade process away from strictly presidential discretion. Partly, that trend has resulted from a congressional emphasis on the economic side of international relations, as opposed to political or military relations.

It can be seen, for instance, in the history of the U.S. trade representative. Originally the State Department exercised those functions; then there was the special trade representative's office established in the White House. In 1979, it was given a statutory basis and

17

renamed the United States Trade Representative, and designated by Congress as the lead trade agency. A similar change in role and increase in functions has taken place in the International Trade Commission.

Again in 1979, the responsibility for administering the countervailing duty and antidumping laws was shifted from the Treasury to the Commerce Department in an attempt to make those two remedies for unfair trade practice quasi-judicial. Congress did not want political or diplomatic factors to weigh on the decisions to the extent that they had in the past.

Underlying these changes has been an enormous shift in the U.S. economy. We are now full-fledged members of the international economy in a way we were not even a decade ago. Then, a gathering of all the trade specialists would probably have fit in one room. Now, it is hard to find a congressional district in which trade is not a matter of interest. It is not always an import problem. A number of the West Coast states, for instance, have an enormous export orientation. Instead of the few congressmen and senators who were once focused on trade, almost everybody now sees it as a problem. They have to respond to local pressures. They have to be more involved.

Finally, the U.S. role in the world was seen to have changed enormously in two hundred years. We came a long, long way from the days when we were largely an agrarian economy, when international trade was of limited interest, when the thrust of our foreign policy was to avoid international entanglements. Suddenly we found ourselves part of the global economy with global responsibilities and with a constitutional system that was not necessarily designed to deal with that reality.

In the attempt to bridge that constitutional gap, Congress has continued to delegate authority and has been willing to adjust its procedures in considering trade agreements. In return, however, it has demanded much greater congressional oversight and involvement, together with a stricter definition of what those trade negotiations will pursue.

We should look at these attempts to reduce presidential discretion in the trade arena in light both of a $170 billion trade deficit and of two longer term trends—the change in the U.S. economy, and the congressional belief that political and diplomatic factors have weighed too heavily where economic considerations should have played a larger role.

4

The Congressional Perspective

Joanna Shelton

The remarks of Alan Holmer and Kent Hughes show how very much in sync the Congress, the administration, and the various committees of Congress are. But there are some other points I would like to cover and highlight. At the outset I would like to stress the Article I, section 8 authorities granted to the Congress to regulate commerce with foreign nations. It is particularly important to remind our trading partners of this when they question why Congress is becoming so involved in trade policy and why Congress is not leaving it to the president. It is important to remind people that this is an authority constitutionally granted to Congress.

Since Kent Hughes has talked about some of the pressures on Congress and why we are wrestling today over precisely how much power and flexibility the president should have under our trade laws, I would like to focus on some of the proposed changes to current trade laws that we made in H.R. 3.

Much debate occurred during the Ways and Means markup of H.R. 3 over the transfer of decision-making and import-relief authority from the president to the U.S. trade representative. We will see over time how this issue plays out. The administration has expressed its opposition to such a transfer, but the committee is comfortable with it. In fact, the number of trade laws in which the committee has proposed a shift in this decision-making authority mean it will become a far-reaching change if enacted into law.

It occurs first in section 301 in those cases in which H.R. 3 would require some type of mandatory response to foreign unfair trading practices. In using the word "mandatory," it is important to note that the Committee granted a national economic interest waiver. If the president thinks the "mandatory" action is not in the national economic interest, he has some flexibility not to act.

In these "mandatory" cases, the Committee transferred decision-making authority from the president to the USTR. The committee adopted that amendment, which is a partial transfer of authority, in the face of an effort to transfer all decision-making authority under section 301 from the president to the USTR. So the transfer was narrowed to just some cases.

The second place that this transfer of authority occurs is in section 201, in escape-clause actions. There, we have the USTR deciding whether or not relief is warranted and, if so, what form it should take.

In section 337, which deals with intellectual property rights violations by imports and other unfair trade practices, we would transfer to the USTR the authority to review and to disapprove ITC determinations and proposed actions.

Finally, we made this change in section 406, which deals with market disruption by nonmarket economy imports. Again, as in section 201, the USTR would have the authority to grant relief and determine the form of relief, within the constraints of the law.

In addition to this transfer of authority, H.R. 3, primarily in Section 301, limits the president's and the USTR's flexibility to act in certain areas. Section 301 as amended carves out a two-track approach. In cases that involve a trade agreement violation or export targeting, an action in response must be taken unless it is not of national economic interest. In other section 301 cases, H.R. 3 retains the discretion currently available to the president in decisions whether to act or not.

With the administration's concurrence, we also imposed a time limit on the president's decisions under section 301. A source of frustration in Congress has been that section 301 is not used frequently enough and that a number of notable cases have dragged on for years with no decision. Both the administration and Congress believe that an industry that has taken the time and money to bring a case deserves a response within a reasonable period of time.

One question raised by these changes, which has been debated within the committee and I'm sure will be debated on the floor and in the Senate as well, is whether this balance is appropriate. Are we weakening the president by shifting authority he currently has to the USTR? Does it make sense from a trade policy perspective?

Clearly the Ways and Means Committee believes the answers are yes, it makes sense, and no, it does not weaken the president's authority. Much of the authority the president currently has is, in fact, delegated by Congress; therefore, if Congress takes back a bit of this authority or circumscribes it, or shifts the actor, that does not seem an undue limit on the president's authority.

As to whether so much of this authority should be vested in the U.S. trade representative rather than in the president, Chairman

Rostenkowski—whose view reflects that of most committee members —has stated on numerous occasions that the United States would be better served by having one voice in trade policy and having trade concerns elevated to a higher level of priority. Kent Hughes alluded to the concern that trade issues tend to take second place to base rights or to other factors. With a deficit the size of ours, many members of Congress believe that the U.S. government ought to give a higher priority to trade policy.

Congress's concerns, however, go beyond the recent frustrations stemming from the trade deficit. Kent Hughes has described the pressures that led to the more than 300 trade bills pending in our committee in the last Congress and that led to passage of trade legislation. However, Chairman Rostenkowski and others have said this trade bill is not being passed for this president. If it is signed into law at the end of this year, only one year will be left in his term, so the law will govern the next president and the one after that. This fact shows that Congress wants to see much greater cohesiveness in trade policy as a general proposition and not just to satisfy immediate frustrations.

My last point goes back to the question whether some of these actions, particularly the transfer of decision-making authority to the USTR, do diminish the president's authority. Consider the following facts. Exchange rate intervention can have a far greater impact on U.S. trade balances than a single trade action against a country here or there. Yet the secretary of the Treasury is the sole actor in those matters. He does not even have an interagency body to consult when he determines whether or not to intervene or whether to pressure foreign governments to lower interest rates, to raise interest rates, or to take other related actions. And when the secretary of commerce makes decisions under antidumping and countervailing duty laws, no one questions whether that diminishes the president's authority. These people work for the president of the United States. It is possible that they may make a decision that is fundamentally at odds with the president's stand. But if they make such a decision once, they probably won't be around to make a decision like that again. The point is that the president's authority is not diminished by having various cabinet officials, including the U.S. trade representative, make decisions on his behalf.

5

Trade Policy and the Trade Representative

William D. Eberle

What we are dealing with today is no different from what we dealt with in 1974, what we dealt with in 1962, and what we dealt with in 1940. It is not anything new. There are just new people.

We are talking about the constitutional privileges of Congress. Yes, it does have those rights, but the executive branch also has some constitutional privileges to negotiate. It has always been difficult to decide where those two lines meet. The fast track was resolved over a three-day period between the trade representative's office and three senators, as a way of allowing the Senate and the House to initiate legislation without giving up their authority. That was the principle that brought about the fast track, which has been in place only thirteen years.

Trade policy today differs in some respects from that of the 1940s and 1950s, but not from that of the late 1960s and 1970s. Trade policy is only one minor aspect in what affects trade. Monetary policy, macroeconomic policy, and fiscal policy have as much to influence as trade policy. They cannot be separated, although this administration has tried to separate them.

In the late 1960s and 1970s, John Connally and I traveled the world tying trade policy, monetary policy, and investment policy together. When I was the trade representative, I was also the head of the Cabinet Council for International Economic Policy. We made a point of bringing things together because, when Congress hears from its various constituents, it hears about their products being overpriced because the dollar is too high or about investments going bad because of the fluctuation in the dollar. That has nothing to do with trade policy.

Leadership in setting trade policy should be distinguished from leadership in enforcement. We have been talking today about the enforcement side—sections 301 and 201 and negotiating authority. They are quite different from the trade policy that Joanna Shelton was talking about. Part of the problem today is the frustration of many congressmen and senators who want to set trade policy but do not want the responsibility for it. Their dilemma is that they are not organized to handle all trade policy and to deal with it in a way that makes sense in negotiations, and yet they have the constitutional authority.

Congress has to decide whether the policy will be implemented by the International Tariff Commission or the trade representative's office or the Commerce Department or the Treasury. Congress will get mad at one agency and give the authority to somebody else, as it did when it transferred dumping out of the Treasury Department. When Congress doesn't like policy, it changes it. I don't think that's too important.

But as Joanna Shelton suggests about the transfer of discretionary powers to a cabinet officer, he will no longer be there if he differs with the president. I can say that in no uncertain terms. Although presidents don't like to discharge people, their staffs do, and they will get it done.

Transferring authority will not solve the problem, but it may leave the president without sufficient discretionary authority. That will create total havoc, in my opinion, in the negotiating ability of any administration. We are not negotiating trade policy all the time—we are negotiating monetary policy. For example, one might say it is an unfair trade practice for countries like Korea and Taiwan to peg their currency to the American dollar. That could be called a trade policy, though it really isn't. Those currencies should be handled in the market, not pegged in an artificial way.

We have the same problem in the so-called monetary side. How many times has the trade representative sat in on the IMF–World Bank meetings? How many times has he conferred with the Treasury secretary on issues? Not since my day has that happened, as far as I know. Until that happens, Congress will be frustrated because those things do influence trade policy. And I would add that Congress has to become fiscally responsible and bring down the budget deficit, which is probably the largest single cause for the trade deficit. Until that happens, we will have this problem.

The leadership in Congress has to indicate to any administration its desires regarding implementation and flexibility, because at least six cabinet members have to be coordinated. Trade policy has to take all that into account. One cabinet officer simply cannot do that.

What we will really need is a National Security Council for trade policy, and that NSC may have to have some responsibility to Congress.

Part Three

What the Numbers Say:
Summary of the Competitive Position
of the United States

6

Overview of the U.S. Competitive Position Today

Allen J. Lenz

My task is to set the stage by defining the problems and putting them into perspective. I see the U.S. trade situation as involving two principal issues: one is the trade deficit; the other is international competitiveness. I see them as separate problems: the trade deficit as transitory and international competitiveness as an enduring challenge. This division is useful because the two problems require essentially different policy treatments.

The right way to look at the U.S. trade situation is to focus not on the merchandise trade balance that is faithfully reported in the newspapers but on the current account. The current account, of course, is the sum of all U.S. external transactions—both goods and services.

The current account of the United States fluctuated around the balance line, alternating between relatively small surpluses and deficits until about 1983, when it began a very steep descent into very large deficits. The deficit was $107 billion in 1984, reached $117 billion in 1985, and was $140 billion in 1986.

A current account surplus, which we have not experienced for several years, means that a nation is producing more than it is consuming, exporting the difference, and lending abroad. A current account deficit means that the nation is producing less than it is consuming, importing the difference, and borrowing abroad. The $140 billion net deficit in 1986 means that we were borrowing at the rate of almost $600 a person from sources abroad.

The current account deficit has become very large relative to the size of the American economy as measured by the gross national product. It was about 2.8 percent of GNP in 1984, 3 percent in 1985, and 3.3 percent in 1986. That is, over the period 1984 and 1986 the United States was consuming each year about 3 percent more in goods and services than it was producing, with net imports and borrowing from abroad making up the difference.

The United States has thus moved quickly from being the world's largest creditor, which it was as recently as 1982, with a creditor position of about $136 billion, to being the world's largest debtor—$220 billion—at the end of 1986. The peak investor position took about 70 years to accumulate; we moved from that position to the position of world's largest debtor in only five years. The debtor position does not pose an immediate problem. We are the largest debtor in nominal terms but certainly not in relation to the size of our economy. Today our debt is about 6 percent of GNP; Brazil's nominally smaller debt is roughly 40 percent of GNP.

Although the debtor position is not a matter of immediate concern, we should be concerned about the longer term. Our debt cannot continue to grow indefinitely at rates of 3.3 percent of GNP or anything near that. Even the United States cannot borrow indefinitely at that kind of rate.

Most projections indicate that our current account deficits will not come down rapidly and that significant net borrowing from abroad will continue for some time. Some project that by the end of the decade we will have a debtor position of some $600 to $800 billion, perhaps $1 trillion in the early 1990s, an amount that would be equivalent to 15 to 20 percent of GNP.

This kind of borrowing cannot and will not continue indefinitely. The growth of debt as a percentage of GNP will be forced by the international economic system, if not by policy actions, to slow, and ultimately, to stop. Current account deficits will be forced by economic conditions to narrow. If necessary, exchange rates, relative international growth rates, and relative prices will change. At some point our debtor position will stabilize and perhaps begin to decline, at least relative to GNP. Policy actions can expedite and smooth the change; but even without policy actions, the international economic system would ultimately force change.

I would like to examine the areas of deterioration in the current account over the past few years to seek some insight into where the improvement—sooner or later—must and will come. There are five principal elements in the current account. By far the largest is merchandise trade, which had a deficit of $147.7 billion in 1986 on a balance-of-payments basis. That is a different basis from the cost, insurance, and freight basis on which the monthly trade data are reported. Merchandise trade was by far the largest component of the deficit.

Business services, a much smaller account, had a surplus of 2.9 billion in 1986. Investment income—the difference between payments that U.S. citizens receive from foreign investments abroad and payments made to foreigners for their investments here in the United States—yielded a surplus of $23 billion in 1986. The smallest account, other goods and services, yielded a deficit of $3.5 billion in 1986. It consists basically of transactions of the U.S. government with other governments. The final account is unilateral transfers—mostly payments to U.S. citizens living abroad who have retired, basically social security payments. It is always negative and will get larger as the number of U.S. citizens living abroad increases and the payments increase.

I want to look in more detail at business services. Because the United States is rapidly becoming a more services-oriented economy, many people think that business services are going to be a solution to our current account problems, that we might eliminate our current account deficits through the export of business services. But that really does not follow.

The business services account is dominated by travel, passenger fares, and shipping. They are the major portion of the account, and they are items on which we typically run deficits.

Proprietary rights—licenses, fees and royalties, the selling of technology, the licensing of technology—yield a surplus. It was $9.6 billion in 1986.

The last item in the business services account is other business services, which is what most people think of as business services. It includes film rentals, fees for consulting, fees for construction abroad, the sale of insurance, telecommunications services, banking services, and the like. The balance is small: a $2.9 billion surplus in 1986. It is usually about that amount.

We are now buying relatively more technology abroad than we have been in past years, and the portion of world patents being granted to U.S. citizens is dropping. While we would hope to make some gains in the kinds of things included in other business services, we are getting very tough competition from Japanese, Koreans, and a number of other competitors. We cannot really expect to make big gains in the balance on business services, and improvements in this small account cannot make a major dent in a current account deficit of $140 billion.

To summarize, what can we expect from the various elements of the current account? Other goods and services typically have a negative balance. As the dollar falls, we should not expect that to improve; it will probably worsen moderately as we have to pay more in U.S. dollars for services the government buys abroad. Unilateral transfers, the payments to social security recipients overseas, will consistently worsen. International investment income can probably go only one way; it too will worsen. It is positive now, but as the United States becomes a larger and larger debtor, it will slip into deficit. We can hope for some improvement in business services, but the amount will be relatively small.

That leaves us with the need to compete internationally in merchandise trade. That will have to be the dominant factor in any improvement.

With that in mind, let us dissect the merchandise trade account. Imports have exceeded exports for an extended period and have grown enormously. Exports peaked in 1981, declined, and then began to recover; but in 1986 total U.S. merchandise exports were still somewhat less than they were in the peak year of 1981.

The merchandise trade account is dominated both on the export side and on the import side by manufactures: 78 percent of our exports and 80 percent of our imports were manufactured goods. On the export side agriculture is 12 percent of the total; on the import side fuels, of which the major item is oil, are down to about 10 percent.

The total trade deficit in 1986 was $169.8 billion, $139.1 billion of which was in manufactures trade. There was a small agricultural surplus of $3.5 billion, down significantly from previous years, and a deficit of $31.7 billion in mineral fuels. Other goods, a small account, includes such items as hides, furs, skins, and wood and paper pulp; in terms of effects in the trade balance, it is not very important, and it does not fluctuate a great deal.

The last time manufactures trade showed a surplus, $10.5 billion, was in 1981. In 1986 it reached a deficit of $139 billion. That is a swing in only five years of almost $150 billion.

Imports, then, have grown very strongly and consistently; exports peaked in 1981, declined, and began to recover. In 1986 manufactures exports were just about 2 percent greater than in 1981. The problem is that manufactures imports were 85 percent greater than in 1981.

The most useful way to look at the account is to examine the swings that occurred between 1981 and 1986. The total deterioration in the merchandise trade account over the period has been $130 billion. The deterioration in manufactures trade was larger, $149.6 billion. The slippage in the balance in the agricultural account was $21.5 billion.

The oil account, however, improved. Oil prices declined, imports declined, and although a deficit remained in 1986, it was smaller by $42 billion than the 1981 deficit.

The important thing is what is going to happen in the future.

What will happen to the fuel account? I think we can expect it to deteriorate again, probably beginning in 1987. Oil prices have firmed; volumes are increasing. The oil deficit is probably going to increase over the next several years.

What is going to happen in agriculture? Are we going to get back some or all of the $21.5 billion? The outlook is not very good. Global food supplies are expanding significantly more rapidly than global food demand. That is the product of a number of factors—the implementation of new technology, the spread of the green revolution to countries abroad, the use of incentives by some governments to promote production, and the increased use of market price incentives in some socialist and less-developed countries. The net result is that many countries that only a few years ago were net importers of food products are now net exporters. Although from year to year we may see modest improvements, we probably cannot expect to get back much of the losses of recent years in agriculture in the near term.

What does that mean? To succeed in international trade, we must balance or come near to balancing our merchandise trade account. That is where we must and will make it. Manufactures trade has been the key variable in the deterioration in the current account in recent years, and it will be the key variable in the improvements that must come.

Geographic analysis of the manufactures trade account shows only a few countries with which we have significant surpluses and a much larger number of countries with which we have major deficits. The largest 1986 deficit was with Japan, $68.1 billion, and we had deficits with four other countries of about $57 billion.

Another way to look at our manufactures trade is on a commodity basis. There are forty product groups at the two-digit level—as we call it in breaking down manufactures products. Only three groups had 1986 surpluses of $2 billion or more, and ten had deficits of $2 billion or more. The largest deficit in the group was in motor vehicles, a deficit in 1986 of $51.9 billion. That deficit in that account expanded from 1985 to 1986 by $12 billion.

Obviously manufactures trade has gone through a very difficult time. What is going to happen? Is the country deindustrializing? Will manufacturing in the United States disappear, or is it going to survive?

About a year ago, *Business Week* ran a cover article asking the question, Will the United States become a nation of hollow corporations? The idea was that the United States might become a nation performing only design, marketing, and financial services and that most manufacturing would be performed abroad. If that happened of

31

course, it would raise substantial national security and other concerns. Therefore, an important question is, Is manufacturing going to survive? Are we going to become a nation of hollow corporations? Our answer to that is an unequivocal no. We are not going to deindustrialize as a nation. Is manufacturing going to survive? Absolutely! How can we be so sure, so unequivocal?

No nation, not even the United States, can borrow indefinitely, can accrue debt at the rate of 3 percent of GNP annually. Sooner or later the current account deficits will narrow and return to something like balance. The question is when it will happen.

In 1985 the United States consumed about 10 percent more manufactures goods than it produced. That left us with a trade deficit of $148.5 billion. Suppose that the movement abroad of U.S. manufacturing continued and that the manufactures deficit continued to deepen to the point where we were consuming 20 percent more manufactured goods than we produced. We would then have a trade deficit of about $260 billion, equivalent to about 6 percent of GNP.

It is our position that such enormous deficits cannot and will not happen; international economic conditions—growth rates, exchange rates, and so on—would preclude it from happening. The United States will not become a nation of hollow corporations. It will not deindustrialize. Indeed, over the long term, the United States will have to export somewhat more manufactured goods than it imports.

The real question about U.S. manufacturing is not whether it survives. The real question is *on what terms* it survives. That means at what exchange rates, at what level of real wages paid to American workers, and how efficient and how productive it will be. That gets into the issue of competitiveness.

To summarize, the trade deficits will decline; manufacturing will survive. That is the good news, but there is bad news too. The more important questions are, When is the trade deficit going to decline? What sort of debt level will be reached before deficits shrink and an upturn begins? How will this come about? What causes deficits to shrink is really a competitiveness issue. Is it going to come about through exchange rate and wage rate declines, or is it going to come about by our becoming more productive, more competitive, more efficient? Last but not least, What happens along the way?

We foresee an extended adjustment process that will affect the United States but will also affect a lot of foreign economies.

Competitiveness is an important issue. Everyone is talking about it, and of course everyone is in favor of increased U.S. competitiveness. But it is not very often defined. The problem with the term, as I see it, is that competitiveness means different things to different observers, and it depends on their perspective.

Competitiveness as seen by an individual firm is its view of its current and projected ability to sell and to profit in international markets or, at a minimum, to compete successfully with foreign firms in the U.S. market. Competitiveness would look very much the same from the standpoint of individual industries. If most of the firms in an industry are competitive in the sense of being able to make a profit and if they are not losing out to foreign competitors in foreign markets or their own market, they would consider themselves internationally competitive.

That is an important point in the sense that the competitiveness of individual firms and industries can perhaps be enhanced by dollar depreciation, by wage cuts, by overseas sourcing of production, and even by U.S. import restrictions. But from a national viewpoint, U.S. international competitiveness has different objectives that cannot be achieved by import restrictions or by inordinate degrees of dollar depreciation, wage cuts, and offshore production.

From a national viewpoint, the objective of international trade is to increase total national wealth and national living standards. The definition of international competitiveness adopted by the President's Commission on Industrial Competitiveness says that a country is competitive if it trades in a reasonably free and open market environment, produces goods and services and trade—and, by implication, balances its accounts—while simultaneously maintaining and expanding the real income of its citizens.

That means that competitiveness is an issue of the standard of living: we need to balance our accounts while *maintaining or expanding* the standard of living of our citizens. We cannot do that by some of the devices mentioned earlier: inordinate wage cuts, dollar depreciation, and so on. At bottom national competitiveness defined this way is a living-standard issue that boils down to a productivity issue, because improving a nation's international competitiveness depends fundamentally on productivity growth rates. That does not mean just increasing productivity; in an integrated world economy, rates of productivity increase must compare favorably with those of major foreign competitors.

There are difficulties in measuring productivity, and no single statistic can tell the story. But one of the best ways to get a quick idea is to look at manufacturing productivity growth rates.

Over the longer term, from 1960 to 1985, the U.S. productivity growth rate of 2.7 percent was lower than those of major industrialized country competitors. For the shorter period 1979 to 1985 it was a little better at 3.1 percent, only slightly below Germany's and better than Canada's. But overall performance has not been good.

For many years after World War II the United States had huge edges over its foreign competitors in technology, manufacturing ability, marketing systems, and the ability to deliver a quality product. It also had access to low-cost energy and raw materials. Enjoying monopolies in many product areas, it was able to balance its international accounts at favorable international terms of trade that supported high and rising U.S. wage levels. But over the years since World War II, the gap between U.S. and foreign competitors has narrowed and in some instances disappeared as foreign capabilities and productivity in some areas have increased more rapidly than our own.

Trade balances will fluctuate, and in time the U.S. trade accounts will return to a sustainable balance. But in a world of rapid technological progress and increasing interdependency, competition from producers in other nations, particularly competition for markets for manufactured goods, will only intensify as foreign production and trading capabilities continue to improve. So the really critical question, which is not going to go away, is, Will the United States be able to maintain an edge in technology, quality, marketing systems, and the like sufficient to maintain or improve U.S. real incomes? And that means, of course, living standards.

What are the key factors in meeting the international competitiveness challenge? There are five elements. We would need high national saving rates sufficient to fund strong capital formation rates, expanding research and development, and continuing human resources development—which means, of course, continuing improvement of the labor force.

We also need effective trade policies, the fifth element. Probably trade policies get more attention than the other elements, those that take a long time to improve. We make an input today and get an output maybe several years downstream. You can balance your accounts without good performance in savings rates, capital formation rates, R&D, and labor force improvement, but you cannot be internationally competitive in the sense that I have defined it without consistently strong performance in these four elements.

Effective trade policies might be defined as a necessary condition. If you cannot get into foreign markets, it doesn't matter how good you are; you will not make much progress. Effective trade policies are a necessary but not a sufficient condition.

Although it may be an oversimplification, it is useful to separate the problems of the trade deficit and of international competitiveness on the ground that they require essentially different treatments. In dealing with the trade deficit, we must do what we can to resolve the debt problem of the less-developed countries, and we need better coordination of international monetary and fiscal policies.

In dealing with U.S. international competitiveness, the important items are laws, rules, and regulations that affect human and physical capital formation and technology development and our trade policies. But common to both would be policies that affect saving, consumption, and investment rates.

In summary I see two major U.S. trade-related problems: the transitory problem of the trade deficit, which we need to reduce to avoid trade-disruptive actions and to minimize growth of the international debt; and the enduring challenge of U.S. international competitiveness, a very important problem because dealing with it is essential to maintaining or increasing U.S. living standards. It is also important to maintaining strong U.S. economic and political leadership.

What lies ahead? The trade deficits will decline. U.S. manufacturing will certainly survive. But the debt is going to grow. The competitiveness challenge is going to intensify. International competition in manufacturing trade is going to get even more intensive than it is now. Part of the solution to our problem will be the movement of foreign firms to the United States to produce here rather than abroad. Adjustment is going to come; there will be major adjustment problems in the United States and abroad. Our deficits will be shrinking, and foreign surpluses will be shrinking. The problems abroad may be even more difficult than the problems in the United States.

Part Four

The Determinants of Competitiveness

7
The Role of Domestic Policy in Addressing Trade Problems

Sven W. Arndt

Political talk in this country conveys the impression that competitiveness is synonymous with trade balances or perhaps even with trade surpluses. Many believe that once we eliminate the U.S. trade imbalance we will have solved the U.S. competitiveness problem. They are wrong, as has been made clear.

The second impression is that all our problems of trade balance and, therefore, all our competitiveness problems, result from unfair foreign trade practices: if we can persuade foreigners to trade more fairly, we will not have any difficulties trading at all. Of course, we all have our favorite target countries that must be brought around to our notion of fair trade.

There can be no doubt that the international trading order needs to be improved and that there are difficulties in the institutional aspects of the system as represented in the GATT. Concern is also justified about the manner in which some countries have exploited the trading system. Even substantial progress, however, toward improving the fairness of trade and achieving many of the objectives that have been expressed by American leaders would leave a major trade balance problem and a major competitiveness problem.

It is worthwhile recalling the rather drastic decline in the U.S. current account, beginning in the early 1980s. Such a decline has got to be caused by some substantial changes somewhere in the system. There is no evidence—and no one has claimed—that trading has became substantially less fair in the 1980s. That is to say, no one has argued that suddenly trading standards seriously declined, or that a rapid major increase in unfairness explains the extreme deterioration in the U.S. trade balance.

Most experts believe that if, for example, Japan agreed to most of our demands for fair trade, we might reduce the bilateral trade deficit between the United States and Japan by something around $7 billion, perhaps even by $10 billion. That, however, would leave a major portion of the bilateral trade imbalance between the two countries unaffected. Other approaches, therefore, must be pursued.

The major reason for the serious decline in U.S. trading fortunes and the trade balance, as distinct from competitiveness, is the macroeconomic policies of the United States. It is, on the whole, generally understood that excess domestic aggregate demand is behind the trade balance deficit. This is reflected in the rapid increase in U.S. imports relative to U.S. exports in the 1980s. The weakness of exports has been attributed to slack foreign demand, but that ignores the supply side. American officials, of course, have done all they can to urge other countries to expand their economies to generate more demand for U.S. exports. They have focused their efforts on Germany and Japan, while at the same time supporting demand-reducing austerity programs in debtor nations.

It is all right to urge the Germans to expand; I think the Germans have many good domestic reasons for expanding. It is all right to urge the Japanese to expand their macroeconomy; the same thing holds there because there are many good domestic reasons why Japan ought to follow more expansionary policies. Although expansion in those countries will obviously help the U.S. trade balance, we could probably achieve more, or at least as much, if we revise our approach to the international debt problem. Our exports to developing countries, especially to debtor developing countries, have been flat lately, for good reason. These countries have been forced into austerity programs designed to limit imports and generate exports so as to generate the foreign exchange needed to service their debt. We have not managed the debt problem in our general interest. It has been good for the banks but not for American exporters, whether in agriculture or in manufacturing. If asked what this Congress and this administration could do to help with the trade problem, I would have them redesign the way that the international debt problem is being managed.

There is, however, another reason for the sluggish performance of exports in recent years: the supply side. One reason, perhaps, why American exports have not grown is that the resources that would normally have produced exports have been needed at home. Domestic demand, relative to output, has grown rapidly, while exports have been held back because resources have been shifted into the production of goods for domestic consumption, both public and private. In fact, a crucial feature of recent macro policies in this country is their effect on the composition of output in the United States, with a very strong bias toward production of nontradables. In the 1980s the price of nontradables relative to tradables has increased rapidly. The relative prices of all sorts of services, construction, and the like have risen. What that suggests to resource owners, to those who make allocative decisions in the private sector, is that they should forsake the production of tradables and move their resources into nontradables, where relative profitability is greater. I would argue that to a significant extent the difference in relative profitability has been caused by U.S. macro policies.

That would also explain why we apparently have such a very long J-curve, such a long lag between changes in exchange rates and corresponding changes in the trade balance. We have dismantled capacity in the tradables sector, shifting resources to nontradables; it will take time to expand capacity in the tradables sector. On top of the normal J-curve effects, therefore, I expect this trade imbalance to take longer to turn around, because across a broad range of manufacturing in this country, there is not the economically efficient capacity that would enable rapid expansion of exports at economically competitive prices.

My view, then, is that it will do Congress no good to imagine that all we need is to force others to change their macro policies. That will help, but that alone won't do it. The administration and Congress must recognize that they have to develop constructive domestic policies—otherwise, they are just deluding themselves. They are also misleading the public by suggesting that improvements in the fairness of trade will solve this country's trade problems.

Even after macroeconomic conditions inevitably change and the trade balance improves, however, a more fundamental problem with competitiveness remains. I believe that in spite of its current difficulties the United States has abundant opportunity to be competitive in manufacturing. Ours will not become a service economy, and it certainly will not become a low value-added service economy. The United States, however, must do more to sustain, maintain, and improve its competitiveness. We must above all strive to improve the quality of our capital and labor resources. We need investment in human as well as physical capital. While we are still a capital- and human capital–abundant country, and can be expected to continue to be competitive in skill-intensive and capital-intensive products, we are losing our edge. The gap between the United States and its skill abundance and capital abundance and those of other countries is narrowing.

The rates of human capital formation, the rates of skill creation, are much faster in some countries, including some newly developing

41

countries like South Korea, than in the United States. That narrows the U.S. advantage and means that in the future other countries will produce their own skill-intensive products rather than importing them from the United States. That means that on the margin some U.S. industries will feel increased competition, first in the markets of these countries and eventually in third markets.

The way to counteract this tendency is to maintain an adequate pace of physical and human capital formation. We have not done that. It is not clear how much can be done in the short run. It is not even clear how much government policy can do in that respect. We do not know what the effects on capital formation of the recently passed tax laws will ultimately be. We do know that the quality, both of labor and of capital, needs to be improved to get desirable productivity increases; that requires a long-term and sustained effort. At the moment, though, no one in Congress, at least, seems to be very concerned with making that necessary effort; there is still the illusion that other countries must do the hard work to correct our trade imbalance and solve our competitiveness problems.

8

The Competitiveness Gap

Gary C. Hufbauer

The competitiveness gap is highly reminiscent of the missile gap. There is something there, but less than meets the eye. In the spirit of this panel, however, I shall concentrate on what is there rather than on what is not. At first sight, the difference between the two gaps is that the missile gap was very narrowly conceived. Who could put the biggest and best satellites up and get to the moon first? By comparison, the competitiveness gap is a fuzzy, ill-defined problem that encompasses almost all our economic sins of omission and commission.

The difference between the two gaps, however, is not so great as that comparison might suggest, because the missile gap was really a metaphor for the balance of military power between the United States and the Soviet Union. Those issues were not put to rest when Neil Armstrong landed on the moon with his crew; they are with us today.

Likewise, the competitiveness gap is, at bottom, a metaphor for the balance of economic power with Japan. The contest with Japan is a long-term contest, and it will not be put to rest by the semiconductor skirmish or by the Trade Act of 1987. As Sven Arndt has emphasized, the contest will not die even if the U.S. current-account deficit disappears and the Japanese current-account surplus disappears.

If we see competitiveness as a metaphor for the economic contest between the United States and Japan, then John Kendrick's recent analysis is comforting but not conclusive. He points out that U.S. productivity growth languished between 1973 and 1981 at about 0.6 percent per year but rose to about 1.4 percent per year between 1981 and 1985. With expansionary monetary policies, productivity could rise, in his view, to 2.1 percent a year between 1986 and the early 1990s. If that prognosis proves true, bringing to an end fifteen years of flat and even declining real hourly wages, the U.S. situation looks much better. But we will still not recapture leadership from Japan in such areas as robotics, fiber optics, and ceramics. Moreover, 2.1

percent productivity growth for the U.S. economy as a whole is at the low end of what Japan has achieved in recent years. For example, the comparison made earlier between growth in the manufacturing sector in Japan and that in the United States for 1979 to 1985 revealed about 3 percent in the United States as opposed to over 5 percent in Japan.

The recent yen appreciation is likely to cause Japan to push even harder on the high-value, high-tech industries. What, then, can the United States do as a nation, and, more specifically, what can trade policies do to address the core of the competitiveness debate?

The prescriptions are relatively familiar. First, savings and capital formation must be stimulated; in the United States they are roughly 16 percent of GNP, whereas in Japan they are about 25 percent. Second, civilian R&D must increase; in the United States it is about 1.5 percent of GNP, in contrast to Japan where it is over 3 percent. Third, the organization of industry should enhance competitiveness.

What do these differences have to do with trade policy? As for the savings issue, the standard macroeconomic story holds that savings are created by the thrifty behavior of the population and that savings are consumed by the profligate behavior of government. That may be an important part of the story but not the whole story. There is a strong two-way causation between export performance and savings. It is not just that savings drive the current account position, but that export policies and export performance affect national savings, particularly that portion of savings always left out of the story: business savings.

Briefly, how does this work? In a high-tech economy, huge costs are essentially fixed, and exports add disproportionately to business profits by spreading those costs over greater amounts of production.

Moreover, in an economy such as Japan's that restrains import competition across a broad range of industries, profit margins are insulated from outside competition. On the one hand, then, the United States, through the absence of a strong export position, has cut decisively into its business savings; on the other hand, Japan, by its internal organization, has added to its business savings. That is obviously not the whole difference in savings between our two nations, but it is a more important difference than has been implied in recent commentary.

As for the second difference, civilian R&D, it is not primarily a question of doing more through the government apparatus. Rather, it is a question of ensuring that firms capture a larger portion of the benefits that accrue from successful R&D. Studies have shown that the benefits of even very successful R&D efforts go largely to the economy and not to the performer of the R&D. If the performer can capture 20 percent of the benefits of a successful project, he is doing quite well. Rules of market organization, patent rules, and trade secret rules affect the ability of a firm to capture the benefits of R&D. I believe the United States is weak in that respect, whereas Japan is strong. Moreover, we are failing to capitalize on our strength if we do not attract the best scientists and engineers from abroad. To put it strongly and somewhat radically, I think that when we give a visa to a foreign student for advanced study in engineering, science, and certain other disciplines, we should also promise him a residence permit upon successful completion of the degree. Further, I believe more opportunity exists to bring in top-flight scientists from Europe, India, and elsewhere who would like to live in the United States.

On the third difference, corporate conglomerates, here again I come back to the issue of very high fixed costs for maintaining position in the high-tech industries. It would be desirable if all high-tech research could be performed by small companies, but I think that is unrealistic. Substantial losses on some products require the deep pockets of very large firms. Under the Reagan administration, anti-trust policy is moving in a favorable direction. But more is needed. In industries where international market competition is significant now and in the foreseeable future, there should be no barrier to mergers within the United States.

9

Successful Exporting:
What the Private Sector Can Do

William Lilley III

Our current competitiveness dilemma is a national problem as big as the inflation or energy problems of the 1970s. In response to those earlier crises, the government undertook a stem-to-stern overhaul of all regulations that, however inadvertently, had the effect of raising prices or encouraging excessive energy use. The government in effect learned that certain regulations enacted for perfectly legitimate reasons had to be altered to accommodate new, unforeseen, but nonetheless compelling national priorities.

In the first chapter of an excellent new book published by the Harvard Business School, *America versus Japan*, the historian Thomas McGraw demonstrates how the Japanese government is organized stem to stern to promote exports. None of our regulations exhibit a similar export orientation. Especially regarding R&D policy, the Securities Exchange Commission, the FASB, and the Internal Revenue Service function as if export expansion were the last thing on their collective regulatory minds. This must change. Our regulations usually reflect a fortress-America mentality because the control of the American market by American companies was a given in people's heads. And, therefore, it did not matter if an American company operated at a regulatory disadvantage vis-à-vis a French company or a German company or a Japanese company.

Of course, this is no longer true now, and if we are serious about our competitive position, we will have to start the unpleasant business of rethinking government regulatory policy. The first flicker of this process is occurring in the tussle over export controls. There intentional regulation is affecting exports. The real work will come when we take on IRS, antitrust, "corrupt practices," and all other laws and regulations enacted for reasons other than exports that nonetheless affect trade.

46

The private sector, however, has the prime responsibility for solving our competitiveness crisis. This is something we have been working on at the American Business Conference (ABC).

The American Business Conference consists of the chief executive officers of 100 high-growth companies. Their firms represent every sector of the economy ranging from Dunkin' Donuts and Hasbro toys to Cray supercomputers. The ABC is somewhat unusual for a Washington lobbying group in that we limit the people who join. And if a company's growth rate falls under 15 percent, its CEO is dropped from the organization, and the CEO of another company comes in. By definition, then, we have exempted from our organization CEOs whose companies have problems competing. At the same time, our selectivity allows us to serve as a sort of "laboratory of excellence" for the policy-making community.

In a recent survey of our members, we found that most were very active internationally and that their rate of success was incredible. Specifically, their internationally derived revenues grew on average per company 230 percent for the past five years. We asked the CEOs to what they attributed that high rate of performance. Almost unanimously, they answered product quality and marketing quality. They argued that the quality issue was pivotal because—and this is a very sharp variance from what we hear in the current political debate—the biggest barrier to the penetration of markets abroad is the perception, true or not, that the quality of American goods and American services is inferior.

The question is, How do we break that quality barrier? Our executives cited attention to detail. They talked about risk taking: breaking into a foreign market takes about four or five years, and a company has to commit itself to losses in that market during that time. They mentioned the importance of R&D investment for both fixed capital and knowledge capital. They talked about the pivotal role of the company leader as either a product innovator or a marketing innovator. And when we looked at their backgrounds, we found that none came out of the chief financial officer stream or the general counsel stream. All of these CEOs had been involved one way or another with innovation of products or innovation of marketing of products.

With the assistance of McKinsey & Company, we then looked at the structure of these companies. The American Business Conference companies are classic entrepreneurial firms in that they ruthlessly make every effort to be nonbureaucratic. Only 20 of the 100 companies have general counsels. These companies have almost no corporate staffs and follow a very hands-on style of management.

47

A number of the executives even went to language schools to learn the language of the country they wanted to penetrate. Let me give you two good examples. One of our most successful companies abroad is Brown-Forman, which is very active selling Jack Daniels, Early Times, and other spirits and consumer products abroad. Jack Daniels is the best selling spirit in Japan, a classic American product, and it took five years of aggressive marketing to convince the Japanese marketplace that this classic American product was desirable. Lee Brown, who runs that company, also has the executive distributorship for Bolla wines in the United States. The Bolla family would not discuss doing a deal with anyone who could not speak Italian. And Lee Brown, a very successful man, took a crash course at a Berlitz school for five weeks to learn to speak Italian.

Two months ago, I got a phone call from John Rollwagen, the CEO of Cray Research, a classic American success company. It was a bad connection. I kept saying, "John, where are you? I can hardly hear you." He answered, "I'm in Paris." I asked, "What are you doing in Paris?" He replied, "Our business plan for 1987 is to sell five supercomputers to the French market, and I have moved my office to the ninth *arrondissement* in Paris to perfect my French to sell them." I inquired, "How big is your office?" And he said, "My secretary." Now that is the kind of nonbureaucratic, hands-on detail that these people think is important if they are to crack these markets.

Two other things came through in reviewing these successes. The CEOs studiously avoid joint ventures in foreign companies. They want to be able to run the business, and they will say that the quality of the product and the quality of the marketing cannot be maintained through some form of committee governance. It also became clear, by the ownership configurations of these companies, that the average amount of stock owned by the top management group is about 40 percent. These executives say implicitly that because the top management controls its own stock ownership destiny, it has insulated itself from the quarterly pressures of financial analysts who can be quite impatient with someone willing to spend five years taking losses to break into an unknown marketplace.

We also asked them, in reviewing the success rate, what lessons had they learned about why they went international. They said they had learned four lessons. The first was that their profit rates are higher abroad in many cases than in the United States because the marketplaces abroad are growing faster than ours. Second, they told us that they went abroad as much to protect their home markets as to find new sources of revenue. Third, in going abroad, they were able to capture foreign technology and innovation and bring it back home.

And fourth, many of them that have moved plants abroad moved them not because of favorable foreign wage rates—these are high-wage companies—but because of cheaper capital sources.

Finally, we asked ABC executives, "What bothers you about the debate going on in Washington that imputes the whole problem, or most of the problem, to the nasty trading practices of foreign countries?" They said that what concerns them most is the attitude—and they see corporate America as being part of it—that the responsibility for opening these markets should somehow be shifted from the heads of American companies to the federal government. Fundamentally, our executives see the task of expanding exports—which is, of course, the ultimate solution to our trade woes—as the task of business. Obviously, government must create a suitable macroeconomic and regulatory environment, but it cannot and, in our society, should not, try to protect business from the realities of world competition. I believe the experience of ABC executives demonstrates that American firms, if they so choose, can meet the challenge of the global marketplace. But it takes work, patience, and, most of all, the unwavering commitment of American management at the highest levels.

Part Five

Trade Legislation, Trade Policy, and U.S. Competitiveness

10

Issues Affecting the Formulation of a Trade Bill

C. Michael Aho

In 1987 President Reagan needs a trade bill if he wants to extend his negotiating authority beyond January 3, 1988, to the multilateral round of the GATT, and even to negotiate with Canada should that not be completed.

When Congress writes trade bills extending negotiating authority there are always, as in 1962 and 1974, amendments to the trade remedy laws or trade statutes. Some people say those amendments are the price that is paid for extending negotiating authority. And I trust the debate today will address the changes in trade remedy laws that will need to be made in the current trade legislative process.

There is quite a bit of congressional frustration with this administration as far as trade policy is concerned. A $170 billion trade deficit and the many different legislative proposals over the past three or four years are two manifestations of that frustration. The desire to change trade remedy statutes is another manifestation.

The sentiment that we ought to toughen U.S. trade laws is widespread. Generally, I think we can see efforts in both the House and the Senate to (1) unilaterally expand or broaden the definition of unfairness, (2) remove presidential discretion under some circumstances, whether or not the president can intervene or, say, reject the advice of the ITC to impose import relief, and (3) mandate retaliation under certain circumstances. In addition, some individuals are proposing that we add mandatory reductions of bilateral trade surpluses over time.

Domestic negotiation over trade policy does not, of course, occur in a vacuum. This negotiation between Congress and the president is being watched very carefully by Japan and the European Community. How will the congressional legislative changes affect the negotiations in the multilateral round of trade talks? And will they perhaps heighten trade frictions?

If, in fact, Congress passes legislation to curb presidential discretion, how much flexibility will that leave for future presidents to deal and to reach negotiated solutions to solving trade frictions and problems?

How will any changes in U.S. laws affect the behavior of other countries? Will those changes in laws be emulated by others and, in fact, turned against the United States in the future when the United States is the country that will have to run a trade surplus in order to service the foreign debt we are so rapidly accumulating? With those questions in mind, we will now hear the views of our six distinguished speakers.

11

Trade Policy: A Democrat's View

Robert T. Matsui

I would like to present the congressional perspective on trade legislation and also on terms of trade generally in the United States today.

In the spring of 1986 the House Ways and Means Committee held a seminar to talk mainly about trade. We invited experts from all over the country, primarily from the academic community, to present their views. One thing I learned from that seminar is that all of us in the U.S. Congress lacked any real knowledge about how the trade deficit actually occurred. Today I find a much greater level of sophistication. Members of Congress have become educated about the whole issue of international trade. And that is not unusual. When an issue first surfaces, we often look at it simplistically; as time goes on, we have an opportunity to find out more about the issue and the underlying currents.

Today members realize that the real problems with our trade deficit are macroeconomic and that any trade legislation passed in the House and Senate and signed by the president will have only a small effect on the trade imbalance itself. Merely opening up markets will not reduce the trade deficit substantially even if we can get buyers and market the products appropriately. The reduction might be $15–20 billion dollars at the very most.

We know what the real problem is, and we know that the president should have been a little bit more aggressive back in May of 1986 at the Tokyo economic summit. Then we could have gotten Prime Minister Yasuhiro Nakasone of Japan and Chancellor Helmut Kohl of West Germany to begin talking about increasing consumer demand in their economies; and we had just passed Gramm-Rudman in late 1985. At that time we would have had some leverage in dealing with the budget deficit.

What did we do at that economic conference instead? We talked about Chernobyl and about terrorism—great for television back home, but we gave up a lot of political capital. Mr. Nakasone finally and reluctantly agreed that yes, Libya was a problem. Although Secretary of the Treasury James Baker tried to salvage something by talking about exchange rates, ultimately that conference was meaningless for international trade.

In terms of the exchange rate at this time, the dollar is going to have to drop more, and there is concern about that. But unless Japan and Germany begin to increase consumption and we get our deficit under control, we will not be able to turn the trade deficit around. That will create the danger of a recession and high inflation.

That is a fundamental problem. When the Democrats and some Republicans were talking about competitiveness during the 1986 election campaigns, we thought we were talking about improving education, the U.S. infrastructure, and so forth.

The trade proposals before Congress do contain those kinds of provisions, but they are long-term provisions and will not have an immediate effect on our trade imbalance. We hope, however, to pass a bill giving the president the authority to be tougher on trade issues.

I would be one of the few Democrats, I suppose, to say that the timing of such legislation is not the best in the world. Perhaps we should allow time to see if, in fact, the J-curve is working. I hope that the Senate will take some time and, by September of 1987, will be in a better position to evaluate the trade legislation.

I am hopeful, however, that we will get a good, sound bill. That leads me to the Gephardt amendment. When we passed Gramm-Rudman in 1985, at least we had the U.S. Supreme Court to bail us out. But in this situation, within the international community, no one will bail us out. The proponents of the Gephardt amendment say they are taking a results-oriented approach to trade. But think about it for a minute. As an alternative approach, the Rostenkowski-Gibbons bill takes away presidential discretion; it requires the U.S. trade representative to find areas of unfair trade practices; it gives the president a period of negotiation—six months or more if he needs it. Then, if agreements do not occur, we have an absolute responsibility to retaliate in kind, unless it's against our national interest. That is about as tough as we possibly can get and still be reasonable from an international point of view. What the Gephardt amendment proposes is dealing with the retaliation by reducing surpluses 10 percent a year beginning in 1989 to a total of 40 percent over a four-year period.

Now, since we have become more sophisticated in Washington about trade, we realize that a trade bill can open up markets, but a trade bill cannot deal with exchange rates, because they are governed by monetary policy. The Federal Reserve and a lot of others—even foreigners—establish monetary policy by determining the amount of money flowing in or out of the United States. What Japan does, what West Germany does, and what we do affects the overall economy and our budget deficit. All of these factors determine whether or not we have a surplus or a deficit.

That we are negotiating to open up markets is really not relevant to the issue of surpluses. In fact, I agree with what Michael Aho said in his opening remarks, that by getting our competitiveness structure back under control, in maybe three or four years we will start generating a surplus.

I must admit that I am a little frightened at what might happen to the Japanese, the Germans, or some of the less-developed countries if we have a surplus: they will probably have deficits. And maybe their economic and international policy makers will decide that countries that have surpluses should be retaliated against.

So I think we're shooting ourselves in the foot. I think the Gephardt amendment is bad economic policy. Not only is it bad economic policy, I believe as a Democrat that it makes absolutely no sense at all. I think the Democrats' opportunities in the 1988 election are great. But for us to go back to a protectionist trade policy makes absolutely no sense at all.

My comments that we have to be sensitive and careful about trade legislation do not mean that I am completely a free trader. Many of you know that I sponsored a telecommunications bill that is in our current trade bill. I believe the Europeans will finally have to begin to be concerned about their consumers, just as we are concerned about ours and that technological advancements will require the Europeans to open up their markets so, for example, their telephone users will be able to use the latest equipment, just as we are doing. We can give the Japanese higher quality rice—and they know it—at probably ten times less cost. But the Japanese are saying they have a political problem: they want to protect their farmers because they made campaign contributions to the Diet members.

And when the Japanese say they can't open the market to U.S. rice because rice is a sacred product, I would only suggest that they label the Japanese rice as having religious overtones and the U.S. rice "Made in U.S.A.," and let the marketplace in Japan decide if the people want to buy higher priced rice for religious reasons.

Our trading partners have a lot of work to do, just as we do. We have to get labor and business and the government to understand a little bit more about our problems. But it is a two-way street, and we will have a lot more problems in the future unless we are willing to work together.

12

The Need and the Prospects for a Trade Bill in 1987

Sander M. Levin

The more I see and the more I read on the trade issue, the more I am convinced that it is probably less a matter of policy than it is of position. The Japanese have a surplus with the United States, with the European Community, and with virtually everybody else. The EC has a surplus with the United States and a deficit with the Japanese. We have a deficit with both and with most everybody else.

The data are startling. Unless you're a purist, unless you really believe that when things get worse they are really getting better, the data are dramatic. The February 1987 figures on manufacturing for the United States were $13 million for exports, $25 billion for imports—for just one month. Our trade deficits over the past years are equally startling: in manufacturing $83 billion in 1984, $107 billion in 1985, $145 billion in 1986, $24 billion for the first two months of 1987.

In the EC literature, the talk about Japan is just as tough as in the United States. If there is not a major turnaround soon, the Europeans threaten to institute a series of tariffs in selected industries to get at the trade imbalance. But as to the United States, the Europeans like the imbalance.

We are called protectionist if we act to reduce our deficit with the EC. We have been captured by our policy in this country, and we are in danger of being captured by our labels. I am impatient if someone from West Germany says we are protectionists while saying that what they are proposing vis-à-vis Japan is somehow free trade.

I think we should not be at all misguided as to what is at stake here. We have a lot to learn from the Japanese. They have made it very clear that the country that controls implementation will control innovation, eventually. The country that controls manufacturing is going to control innovation and high technology.

I agree with the senior management director of Toyota who said,

"You can't survive with just a service industry." Perhaps Bob Matsui and I are so outspoken in our differences on these issues because he is from California and I am from the Midwest. I do not say that to diminish our positions one iota, but those who are suffering are likely to be the most active in expressing it and wanting action.

The problem that everybody should understand is that the decline in competitiveness is not only in the Rust Belt; it is not only in the shoe industry of Maine; it is not only in the textile industry of the South. It has spread throughout the United States. It includes a number of high-tech industries; it includes telecommunications. In my judgment, we have to address all of the industries and all of the sectors that are in peril, not just one.

It is nothing new that people do not take action before they are forced to, particularly when they are ahead. We probably do it in our households every year, if not every month, if not every week. That is what I believe the debate is about in the U.S. Congress today.

I do not put much emphasis on the shift of authority in the House bill from the president to the U.S. trade representative. I don't mean to diminish the significance of the amendments Congress is considering. We fought over them. But any president worth his salt is going to control the U.S. trade representative. It may be somewhat important to elevate the status of the trade representative, but it is not a major shift.

The fight in Congress is mostly about opening up markets. But let no one say that I am suggesting that doing so would be a cure-all. There is none. But opening up the markets of other countries has some significance, some psychological significance and more.

The House Ways and Means Committee bill says if one of our trading partners has a trade surplus with us of 75 percent and we detect a pattern of unfair trade practices, the United States must initiate negotiations. If those negotiations fail, or if an agreement is reached but it does not bring any result, the president must take action to reduce the surplus, in essence, by the value of other nations' unfair trade practices.

The Gephardt amendment requires a reduction in the surplus of 10 percent a year *as long as the pattern of unfair trade practices continues.* Those who oppose the amendment overlook the waiver authority of the president that is essentially the same in the Gephardt amendment as it is in the Ways and Means Committee proposal. The president can waive the Gephardt procedure if it is not in the economic interest of the United States. There can hardly be any broader authority.

If it ever occurs that our imports to the EC exceed their exports to us by 75 percent and they don't get up on their hind legs and howl, there is something wrong with the EC. If we had a $50 billion trade surplus with the Japanese, they would automatically organize a massive effort to correct that imbalance, as well they should. What the Gephardt amendment says is that we simply must empower ourselves in this country to force change. We cannot continue to allow industry after industry to be unfairly hurt. As I said before, the control of basic industry in the long run means the control of innovation.

I will close with some examples of what is happening in the auto parts industry. A couple of years ago Japan was selling $13 billion worth of automobiles to the United States. How much were they buying in the way of auto parts from the United States and every other country? Less than $125 million. We sparked in Congress some interest in talks on auto parts, but the tremendous imbalance has continued. Our trading competitors, the Japanese, who are our allies generally, cannot even agree with us to monitor trade levels, let alone set some kind of goal.

Changing the currency exchange rate will not by itself remedy the imbalance. It hasn't worked before, and it is unwise to put so much emphasis on any single solution.

The trade imbalance is also not a matter of presidential politics. Even if the presidential election were four years away, the situation would be the same. Fortunately, there is a new attitude in Congress and a new mood in the country: down with theory and up with results. I think the Congress of the United States will produce results in 1987.

13

Trade Policy: A Republican's View

Tom DeLay

I believe that if the Democracts pass the Gephardt amendment the results will do nothing but elevate the Republicans in the eyes of the consumer. I am concerned that the passage of the trade bill will cause international economic catastrophes the likes of which we have not seen since the Smoot-Hawley Tariff Act was one of the causes of the Great Depression.

Although this latest round of trade protectionism is ostensibly aimed at foreign targets, the real cost of such trade wars comes back home in the form of higher prices, reduced availability of desired products, lower standards of living, and lost job opportunities. This false and costly bill of protectionist goods is being peddled by Congress into the pockets of the American consumer.

I can assure you that the United States is not losing the competitive battle with any other country. We are by far the most competitive country on the face of the earth. We control over three-fourths of the computer software market, up from two-thirds. We hold about 70 percent of the world computer market. Domestic textile production has risen more than 20 percent since 1985, a rate five times faster than the overall growth in U.S. manufacturing.

Since 1981, output per hour in manufacturing has grown at an average rate of 3.8 percent, more than twice the annual rate of 1.5 percent recorded between 1973 and 1981. In my judgment, and that of most leading economists, this productivity increase has been a direct result of U.S. industry competition with the so-called flood of foreign imports. Without these imports, I doubt that we would have seen anywhere near these gains in productivity.

Our country is plenty competitive, but unfortunately, the loudest voices are those of industries that are losing their competitive edge to overseas suppliers for one reason or another. The result is that many of our leaders have started blaming other countries for our inability to compete with their efficient industries. We scorn them for making better quality cars and cheaper shoes. And rather than allowing our consumers to enjoy these economic benefits, we shut down our markets, maintain our inefficiencies or worsen them, and pile the costs onto the American consumer.

The consumer costs associated with protection on goods imported into this country are immense and hurt the poorest segments of our population. For a family making $50,000 a year, protectionism costs about 2.7 percent of their income. But it takes away a whopping 32 percent of the purchasing power of the family that is just at or above the poverty level. That was a cost of $121 billion to American consumers between 1984 and 1986.

For steel, the costs to the consumer of import restraints were $114,000 for every $29,000 job saved. Voluntary restraint agreements with the Japanese on automobiles cost you and me $241,000 for every $27,000 job saved. The sugar program costs us $53,000 for every $19,000 job saved, and now the new trade bill might contain a provision to start protecting candy bars, because we cannot seem to compete with foreign candy made with cheap foreign sugar.

The most common myth surrounding the trade debate seems to be that imports cost jobs and that trade deficits indicate poor economic performance. Between 1983 and 1986, however, the years of our highest trade deficits, we created five times as many jobs as Japan and a hundred times as many jobs as West Germany, both of whom have trade surpluses with us.

The United States has been enjoying its second largest and the longest period of economic expansion since World War II. At the same time, however, the recovery of economic activity in most other foreign countries has been weak. The result has been that we have purchased and imported far more than at any time in our history, and we have been exporting less because of weak overseas markets.

During the first six quarters of our current expansion, total domestic demand grew much more rapidly in the United States than in any other country. Since then, the differences have narrowed, but a large cumulative gap in domestic demand growth remains. At an accounting level, the U.S. deficit signifies that the total expenditures on goods and services in the U.S. exceed U.S. production of goods and services and that the United States is importing the difference.

How anyone can take this to mean that we are having economic problems is hard for me to imagine. These are natural growing pains associated with a strong economy. What I think lies behind all of the criticism of current trade policy is the quest for an issue for the 1988 elections. The Democrats want to get Ronald Reagan's economic growth policies out of the White House and to restore the economic stagnation and misery of the past. It absolutely confounds me that a trade bill like H.R. 3, known by those who share my views as the Trade Reduction and Job Destruction Act of 1987, could possibly get the support it is getting. People at the Brookings Institution on one end, the Heritage Foundation on the other, and the American Enterprise Institute all are saying that protectionism does not save jobs or help the economy.

A recent Brookings Institution study found that the voluntary export restrictions, which were supposed to increase employment in the U.S. auto industry, have actually reduced it. The study goes on to say that these effects could have been anticipated if careful economic analyses had been performed before legislation was initiated.

Unfortunately, most of my colleagues would say, "Don't confuse me with the facts." This is exactly what is about to happen in the U.S. House of Representatives, where we are probably going to pass a trade bill. Mr. Gephardt says he has the votes to pass his protectionist amendment. God help us if he does. And all of this is amid thousands of studies showing that these types of actions do not work, have never worked, and never will work.

Time and time again history has shown this, but the House is going to pass a bill anyway. It is an emotional issue. Facts are not emotional. And if the administration's minuscule tariff action affecting less than $300 million worth of goods could cause the stock market to take the second largest plunge in history, just watch what happens if we pass the Gephardt amendment.

I think this country is missing a prime opportunity to make changes that really affect our competitiveness. I am proud of this country and of our ability to compete. I think we should quit whining about how unfair everybody is to us and start putting our economic engine to work. The way we do this is to unshackle U.S. businesses from the burdens of obtrusive government. On the very top of the list is reducing the federal budget deficit.

Paul Volcker said in a Senate Banking Committee hearing that neither a cheaper dollar nor sweeping protectionist measures would cure our trade deficit problems. He said the most important thing to do is to reduce the federal budget deficit and thereby cut the flow of capital from other countries to the United States; if that capital inflow is reduced, the trade deficit will be too.

This number one issue is obviously on the bottom of the list for the leadership of Congress. They are trying to loosen the Gramm-Rudman targets and then raise taxes to achieve higher targets. If our budget deficit problem is not taken seriously, we will never make any headway on reducing our trade imbalance.

Another positive way we can increase our competitive edge is by scaling back antitrust restrictions. The U.S. economy suffers from a range of self-inflicted regulatory restrictions on voluntary arrangements that could otherwise advance economic welfare. As businesses attempt to adapt to fluctuating global markets, changing consumer demands, and new tax laws, the federal government, to protect the consumer, clamps down on these efforts to adapt. Antitrust itself has become a restraint on trade.

Efficient financing is essential for a competitive economy. The failure of Congress to modernize our banking laws, however, is one of the major reasons why the United States is slipping as a provider of worldwide financial services. Only one American bank remains among the world's top ten banks.

Finally, the competitive rationale for freeing the U.S. economy through deregulation has now become obvious. The limited deregulation of truck, airline, and rail industries has resulted in transportation and logistic cost savings on the order of $100 billion annually. As we look into the future, we can expect comparable savings resulting from deregulation of financial services and telecommunications.

Akio Morita, chairman of the Sony Corporation, was recently asked: What advice can you provide to help us reduce our trade deficit? And he responded that our industry needs more relief from government regulation in order to restore our worldwide competitiveness.

If we in Congress can take positive steps like these, we can make great gains in reducing our deficit and ensure a rock-solid and permanent position of global productive preeminence.

14

Competitiveness and Trade Policy: A View from the Administration

David A. Walters

The Reagan administration is very concerned, and has been concerned from its beginning, with the competitiveness and performance of the U.S. economy. Trade policy, however, is only one element influencing competitiveness. Other government policies and individual and private effort also influence the competitive performance of the country.

Competitiveness seems to mean different things to different people. Although it is a slippery term, we cannot avoid trying to define it if we are going to formulate policies to improve it. Unless we are clear about the definition of competitiveness, those policies are going to be very ill informed.

Let me give a tripartite definition of where I believe our competitiveness concerns are. First, the trade deficit is, of course, a major concern for many people when they consider the issue of U.S. competitiveness. Our large trade deficit is seen as an indication of failing U.S. competitiveness. In one sense, they are right: it largely represents a loss of price competitiveness in international markets, largely through the strong appreciation of the dollar in the first half of the 1980s, with the attendant accumulation of foreign debt. The trade deficit problem or, more appropriately stated, the current account deficit, is open to adjustment largely through macroeconomic policy measures. It is not open to adjustment through trade policy measures. Using trade policy to fix aggregate trade deficits is really a misuse of trade policy and is likely to result in far more damage than good.

The second concern with competitiveness is competitiveness in the fundamental sense. I have heard competitiveness referred to at times as a question of relative productivity performance. How well is the U.S. worker doing in comparison with workers abroad, given our investment in physical capital, human capital, and new knowledge?

65

Certainly these are aspects of competitiveness, but I would not put excessive weight on what current statistical measures indicate about the performance of U.S. productivity relative to foreign productivity. First, 70 percent of U.S. workers are in the service industries, and our data on measuring productivity in services are poor. The overall mediocre levels of worker productivity in the United States are the average of continued strong performance in manufacturing and of very poor performance in services. The poor performance in services, however, may represent, in part, the inadequacy of our current system of measuring output trends per hour of work by service industry workers. Second, all other things being equal, a country that increases employment five times, ten times, or a hundred times more than other countries—although the tremendous growth in employment is good for the economy because it increases output—may in a statistical sense reduce the measured productivity of the country.

Imagine that tomorrow morning an unemployed, unskilled worker finds a job. His new employment raises national output and per capita income. But, if the next day the statistical measure were to be taken of U.S. *average* labor productivity, we would find that labor productivity had fallen slightly. This would be so because with productive capacity below the national average, the unskilled worker's new employment would, in a statistical sense, slightly depress the national average.

Ironically, in this case a drop in labor productivity is associated with something we consider to be good for the economy, not bad. So, again, it's better to have higher labor productivity growth rates than lower productivity growth rates, all other things equal. But you don't want strong productivity growth at the expense of inadequate job growth or even reductions in employment, as some European countries have experienced in the 1980s at certain times. In this latter case, strong growth in productivity and real wages by those with jobs is associated with growing numbers of people without jobs and sluggish growth in overall output.

The third area of competitiveness that I think is a major concern to many people is commercial policy. For a given state of U.S. economic fundamentals, the ability of our workers and our firms to enjoy the benefits of their investment in physical capital, in human capital, and in new knowledge can be influenced by the commercial policy environment. On the one hand, there are ways countries can enact policies that actually constrain the ability of their firms and workers to move toward producing what they do best. On the other hand, the commercial policies of some foreign countries can unfairly hamper their ability to fully exploit their comparative advantage in international markets.

The administration has attempted to address all three of these senses of competitiveness and has had many successes along the way. It has bills and legislation pending in Congress to make even further progress. For the correction of the aggregate trade deficit, the administration puts most of its emphasis on macroeconomic policies. In the Administration Statement on International Trade Policy of September 1985, reducing federal spending and budget deficits were named as principal domestic actions for increasing gross domestic saving, reducing net inflows of foreign capital, and reducing the aggregate trade deficit.

Improving the macroeconomic climate abroad has also been the object of administration policy for the past couple of years. The Plaza Agreement, also in September 1985, was the first of a series of agreements on international macroeconomic coordination. The emphasis in the Plaza Agreement was, of course, exchange rates, and certainly a lot of progress has been made in reducing the value of the dollar and in increasing the price competitiveness of U.S. products. The Plaza Agreement and subsequent agreements have also been exchanges of statements of macroeconomic policy intentions, basically, for the United States to reduce its federal budget deficit and participants from Europe and Japan to increase their rates of growth in domestic demand.

Data on real trade volumes is beginning to show progress in correcting current trade imbalances. The constant dollar series from the national income and product accounts shows that U.S. exports have grown at an annual rate of roughly 16 percent since the second quarter of 1986. Real imports peaked in the third quarter of 1986 and have since been falling at a 5 percent annual rate. The problem has been, however, that the nominal trade deficit has not shown a similar improvement because rising prices have kept up the value of imports, even as the volume has fallen.

Similarly for Japan, changes in real trade volumes suggest the beginning of a movement toward reduced trade surpluses. Japanese imports, the International Monetary Fund has just reported, increased roughly 12.5 percent in real volume in 1986. Manufactures may have increased more than that in Japan. Their real exports were down 1.5 percent.

With respect to fundamental competitiveness, I agree with Congressman DeLay's statement that the pessimism in product performance over the past five years has been exaggerated. One statistic is particularly interesting: Despite the U.S. slip from a position of surplus in manufactures trade to a deficit of $148 billion last year, U.S. manufacturing output has grown faster than the GNP. From 1980 to 1986, real manufacturing output is up about 19 percent; total GNP is up about 15 percent. If you measure it from 1982, the bottom of the recession, real manufacturing output is up 25 percent, and real GNP is up 16 percent.

So despite, or maybe because of, as Congressman DeLay said, the tremendous competitive pressure being put on U.S. manufacturing firms from what was a very high value of the dollar and the deterioration of the aggregate trade balance, output performance of manufacturing has been substantial in the past five years.

I believe that the role of goverment, with respect to fundamental competitiveness, is to achieve the general economic policies which help maintain the incentives for workers and businessmen to compete to produce the goods and services most desired by the public at the lowest possible price.

Much that the administration has done has been aimed at that — the whole movement toward deregulation and the reductions in marginal tax rates, for example. There is always room for improvement, however. The president's Trade Employment and Productivity Act recently sent to Congress looks at many areas of government involvement with the economy to see where further modifications can be made to improve U.S. competitiveness.

There are many possible strategies—for instance, reducing export controls, reforming product liability regulations, and strengthening the protection of intellectual property rights.

The bill also contains provisions to better facilitate adjustment. Growth inevitably means change. Change in the context of economic growth means that some industries do better than others. Problems are created, particularly for workers, when they find themselves through no fault of their own caught in a sector that is not flourishing.

The president's bill has nearly $1 billion for adjustment assistance, which is aimed at helping workers make the transition toward the jobs and professions that in the future, given the evolving structure of our economy, will offer more promising rewards.

Finally, the bill contains several elements directly pertaining to international trade. These include congressional legislation to facilitate U.S. participation in the new Uruguay Round of multilateral trade negotiations, and to strengthen various elements of U.S. trade law to assist administration efforts to further open foreign markets to U.S. exports.

Let me close by reminding the group that the administration has been working very hard to remove foreign barriers and distortions to trade. The administration also wants to work closely with the Congress on a competitiveness package that complements these efforts. Some elements of current trade legislation that would severely restrict international trade with tariffs and other barriers, however, could damage U.S. and global prosperity. Responsible trade legislation, on the other hand, should foster trade and growth, while congressional action to limit federal spending growth and to further reduce the budget deficit are a principal domestic means for reducing the U.S. aggregate trade deficit.

15

Trade Legislation: A View from the European Community

Sir Roy Denman

A very distinguished member of the U.S. Senate once told me that there should be an illuminated sign over the Capitol telling foreigners they have no vote. But we do buy quite a lot of American goods. The interesting thing for a foreigner living here is that the ghost of the Smoot-Hawley Tariff Act is reappearing at a time when the American stake in overseas trade is far greater than it has been.

For something like a hundred years after the Civil War, foreign trade was never more than 4 to 5 percent of American GNP. Now it is 12 percent and rising. One-fifth of American industrial production is exported, 40 percent of your farmload gross. This is not a time to throw a large wrench into the international trading mechanism.

I come to another point. One hears from time to time that this provision or that provision would not be compatible with the GATT or the international trade rules. Some of my friends ask me, of what use are these international trade rules? They only mean that good old Uncle Sam plays by them; no one else does. Of what use is the GATT except to a lot of bureaucrats in Geneva?

The answer can be given simply in two figures. First, since 1950, just after the GATT started, the volume of world trade has gone up by a factor of seven, American exports in volume terms by a factor of five. American exports have gone up because the United States has some very tough and able businesspeople and farmers. But it also had some tough characters in the 1930s when world trade was strangled like jungle weed and everyone was poor.

Second, between 1950 and 1986 the GNP of the United States went up by a factor of three in volume terms, and foreign trade made a tremendous difference, too.

Legislation enables the government to take foreign trade into account and also to watch out for its own interests. Five million American jobs depend on exports.

Let me deal very quickly with some of the illusions that cluster around the subject of the trade deficit like moths around a candle. First, can you deal with a trade deficit by legislation? Not sensibly. A trade deficit is the result of macroeconomic policies, of exchange rates, of how competitive industry is. The Reagan administration says the major cause of the trade deficit is the budget deficit, but that does not imply that all the evils of the world are in Washington.

In Europe we have a hideous unemployment problem—approximately 17 million people are unemployed. It is a disgrace, and we have to do something about it and about our growth rate. It is a question of taking macroeconomic responsibilities; and dealing with the trade deficit by legislation simply means, to put it crudely, bashing farmers. The French have a proverb: This animal is wicked; when attacked, it will defend itself. You will find that foreigners will defend themselves as well. But getting into a dispute of that sort, given the stake foreign trade now has in the American standard of living, does not seem well advised.

Another illusion has to do with unfair trade practices. Long experience has taught me that in every country of the world everyone thinks what he is doing is absolutely fair and above board, and it is the other guy who is engaging in unfair trading practices. An eminent British businessman complained vigorously to me years ago about the wickedness of Americans and Germans and dumping. So I said, "Don't you ever dump yourself, sir?" "No, no," he said. "I leave nefarious practices like that to foreigners." I said, "What about the report in the press a few weeks ago?" And he said very notably, "Well, not again. I export at a loss in the national interest." He believed what he was doing was perfectly fair.

In 1986, the Office of the U.S. Trade Representative issued a list of unfair trading practices overseas. In the spirit of hopefulness, the European Community has distributed a document listing some thirty American practices that impede trade. We did not do so with any hostile or aggressive intent, but simply to point out that unfair trading practices are not limited geographically to west of Alaska or east of Cape Cod.

These are some of the considerations to keep in mind when looking at legislation. We think in Europe that the Gephardt conception of mandatory action in response to trade deficits or surpluses is not in your own interests. Consider, for example, 1981 when the United States ran a trade surplus with the EC of something like $18 billion. Had anyone come to my office in Brussels and complained about that, I would have ushered him briskly to the door. I would have said, "if they are running those surpluses, it is a combination of various macroeconomic factors and exchange rates, and they may be making a lot of better goods than you boys are. So get to it and sell." We have arguments with our Japanese friends, whose market we do not think is completely open; but apart from particular practices, the United States and the European Community are pretty open markets. If we can each deal with some of our macroeconomic problems, then the situation will right itself without bringing a major hammer to bear on the international trading mechanism.

What are other problems? For one, a tendency to rewrite the internatonal trading rules unilaterally. Now, one of the virtues, I think, of the new round of trade talks in Punta del Este is that it is multilateral. We cannot, of course, set international trade rules in concrete for the next hundred years. But if we go to try to improve, say, the rules on subsidies or dumping, let's improve them multilaterally by agreement. The international trading rules are not perfect, but they're the only international trading rules we've got.

We are facing the prospect that legislation will restrict imports of textiles, which would counteract the Multi-Fiber Agreement. The agreement has been attacked now and again in the press but has provided a stable basis for world trade in textiles over the past twenty years. Changing it would invite retaliation from overseas. If tariffs are going to be placed on European exports of textiles to the United States, then make no mistake about it, the EC will retaliate just at the time when, with the dollar going down, U.S. exports of textiles to Europe are rising quite sharply.

It is, of course, for you to determine what kind of legislation you pass. All we would say as friends and trading partners is, think about some of the consequences for American jobs. Five million American jobs depend on exports. If you take a two-by-four to foreigners, human nature being what it is, they'll take a two-by-four back, and jobs will be lost in districts and states across the union.

16

Trade Policy: A View from Japan

Ryozo Hayashi

First, as almost all economists agree, trade practice and trade legislation have almost nothing to do with current percentage imbalances. In
1978, right before the second energy crisis, the yen rate was 175. If it
had stayed at that level, we might not be facing our current trade
problems. When the energy crisis occurred, reflecting the U.S. "surplus" and the Japanese "deficit," the yen went down to 250. We had
been warning the United States that the high level of the dollar would
surely create an imbalance later on, but in those days, the United
States believed the high dollar was a sign of strength. When the
imbalance started occurring, Japan took several so-called market-
opening measures responding to U.S. requests. But despite the further opening of the market, Japan's surplus increased further, and the
U.S. deficit also increased, because of the growth rate difference and
the exchange rate itself and the decline in prices of commodities, such
as oil and agricultural products. In this context, it should also be noted
that Japan is the second or third lowest major industrial country in
terms of dependency on exports. Our reliance on exports is about 10
or 12 percent.

Change started from the Plaza Agreement of 1985, where exchange rates were readjusted and macro policy started being coordinated. Now, our exports have decreased 4 or 5 percent in volume, and
the import of manufactured products has increased more than 20
percent in volume. These changes have been accomplished by adjustment to the industrial structure. Many steel mills and major aluminum industries are closed down. These adjustments are under way
now. It is these macroeconomic factors that created imbalance and
that can restore the balance.

Unless we succeed in policy coordination we may face some of
the conditions of the 1929 depression: low commodity prices over
capacity, instability of the exchange rate market, lack of leadership or
willingness to have leadership among the major countries, and very

high stock prices. While we are discussing "unfair trade practices," not the real causes of the problem that we are facing now, the world economy may be going over Niagara Falls.

Second, on microeconomic issues, given the expansion of world trade, it is not surprising that some people have succeeded and some have failed. No country can claim that it has completely open markets. Further, fairness, unless agreed multilaterally, is a standard that differs from country to country and even in the same country from time to time.

It is easy to call others "unfair" on the basis of claims by those who fail to sell. But if you spent a year in Japan you would see a tremendous number of successful U.S. companies there. Some studies show that the amount sold in Japan by U.S. companies is equal to the amount sold in the United States by Japanese companies. This has been shown in research done by Dr. Keniichi Ohmae.

You would also notice that in Japan the high level of competition produces customers and consumers who can be very demanding. If a consumer has trouble with an electric appliance, he calls the dealer. The dealer comes to the house and fixes it right away or brings along a replacement.

Consumers of business products expect the same standard. So it becomes a very strong incentive for the manufacturers to reduce repair costs by keeping an eye on quality. The business operation or factory automation is based on a narrow range of differences among the quality of products and services delivered.

The claim of U.S. manufacturers that they cannot sell products in Japan as well as in the United States may be true. It is also true, though, that Japanese customers say U.S. manufacturers can never really come up with the products they want. This is the nature of the market there and cannot be solved by claiming the Japanese are "unfair."

I believe that the economy of the United States can revive itself. This country has tremendous strengths. In order to keep the Western countries competitive and make the future prosperous, it is essential to focus on real problems and underlying economic forces. If politics prevails, it will hurt not only the international economic system, but also the unity of the Western countries by destroying the good will among ourselves.

Part Six

Industrial Adjustment:
Industrial Policy Revived?

17

Reform of Section 201 Import Relief

Don J. Pease

I want to discuss industrial adjustment in the context of H.R. 3, and specifically in the context of the changes Congress is likely to make this year in section 201. The question is, Is industrial adjustment really industrial policy revived or industrial policy in sheep's clothing?

The provision of 201 import relief is itself an act of industrial policy. When the federal government imposes tariffs or quotas in a 201 case, it has taken an action specifically designed to alter the economic course of an entire industry. What is at issue, then, is not whether we should get involved in industrial policy in section 201 but how to improve the industrial policy that is already implicit in the statute.

In its present form section 201 is an unbalanced instrument of industrial policy in two respects: First, when an industrial policy is implemented by an act of Congress, society pays for that action through higher taxes. In return for their tax dollars, taxpayers, through the political process, have some control over the implementation of that policy, a degree of quality control.

I suggest that there is no corresponding quality control for those who foot the bill for industrial policy under section 201. It is not the taxpayer but the consumer who pays. In return for paying higher prices, consumers have every right to expect that genuine adjustment will take place, that the industry will not make further demands on them at the end of the program. In its present form, however, section 201 has little in it to reassure consumers that the industry receiving relief will be able to stand on its own feet after the import protection has expired. The statute is simply not structured to ensure that genuine industrial adjustment will take place; that is, that consumers will get what they pay for when they pay those higher prices.

Second, when people talk about industrial adjustment in 201 cases, they usually mean restoring the financial health of the companies—of the companies, I would underline—in the industry. No doubt this is of central importance; however, if the success of industrial adjustment can be measured by whether the industry presses for yet more special protection after import relief expires, a concept of adjustment limited to corporate profits is seriously inadequate. Balance sheets don't vote; people vote.

If the human component of import relief—worker and community dislocation—is not explicitly and adequately addressed in a 201 relief program, genuine industrial adjustment will not take place. It is likely, indeed, that Congress will be lobbied for further protection.

The House Ways and Means Committee contribution to H.R. 3 addresses both these problems; the Senate bipartisan bill addresses only the first. Because this is what most people have in mind when they think of industrial policy, I will focus only on the first issue: How can genuine industrial adjustment be institutionalized in the section 201 process? How can consumers be assured that they will get what they pay for? In focusing on this issue, I want to assure you that I do not intend to lose track of the second issue: What happens to adjustment of communities and individual workers?

The House and the Senate bills seek to answer these questions about the ability to institutionalize industrial adjustment under section 201 by enhancing the accountability of the industry receiving 201 relief. The industrial policy controversy and the distinction between the current House and Senate bills lie in how and to what extent the industry is made to account for the adjustment measures it will take during relief.

H.R. 3 gives petitioners the option of submitting a statement of proposed adjustment measures. There are no specific requirements about who should formulate the statement or how it should be formulated. The bill simply provides an open-ended opportunity for petitioners to come forward of their own accord and bolster their case by detailing what they intend to do with the relief they seek.

Although H.R. 3 does not require the industry to make itself accountable to society for the relief it receives, it does include a strong, if not obvious, incentive for the industry to do so. The national economic interest waiver in current law has been tightened up by the bill to permit the U.S trade representative to refuse to grant relief recommended by the International Trade Commission only if it determines that relief would threaten national security or if it demonstrates in a substantive economic analysis that import relief would impose greater economic costs than benefits on the nation. Accordingly, the more clearly the industry develops its statement of proposed adjustment measures, the better its chance to influence the cost-benefit analysis on which the import relief decisions will be made.

The Senate bill, by contrast, contains a mandatory, more formal process. It requires that an industry adjustment plan be drafted and submitted by the petitioner, usually as a product of a tripartite working group. The plan would include a broad range of actions that companies, workers, and government agencies can be expected to take during the period of import relief.

Last year the House bill included a similar, though optional, approach, but the House Ways and Means Committee encountered resistance to a formal adjustment plan process. There was criticism that it would be infeasible and undesirable for a central plan development group to make specific investment or restructuring decisions, especially in a large, diverse, decentralized, or nonunionized industry. It was felt that, in the interest of efficiency, decisions about who should expand or retrench in which lines of business should be left to the market.

In February 1987 I introduced H.R. 1308, which, in addition to proposing the cost-benefit analysis refinement to the 201 waiver—which has found its way into H.R. 3—sought to bridge the gap between the formal adjustment process and the status quo. It maintained the tripartite group but altered its responsibilities. Rather than having industry and labor representatives detail the actions they plan to take, it required the tripartite board to agree explicitly on whether the industry as a whole should expand or shrink, invest or restructure.

Specifically, my bill would require management and labor to estimate the size of the industry that would be consistent with its viable operation after import relief had expired and adjustment measures had been fully implemented. The design of specific measures or actions would be left to the companies and unions to work out through normal channels, although their intentions would be communicated to the government representative on a confidential basis. For the purposes of the tripartite group, only an assessment of the appropriate size of the industry and the statement of industry-wide adjustment objectives—not specific company or union objectives—would be required.

In other words, the tripartite group would be responsible for determining the broad benchmarks by which its progress in carrying out industrial adjustment could be judged. It would not be responsible for hammering out a central plan of specific company and union actions. In keeping with American tradition, these would be left to the marketplace. In essence, management and labor would construct the standards to which they would be held accountable. After all, greater responsibility by the industry, not greater involvement by government in the economy, is what we are after in reforming section 201.

One of the great questions of the day is which of these three approaches will be followed. Will it be H.R. 3, the House Ways and Means Committee bill? Will it be the Senate bill? Or will it be the superior product proposed by me earlier this year? All Washington is on tenterhooks waiting for the answer to that question.

The answer is likely to be a little anticlimactic because the three have many similarities. If one examines all three, one can get a pretty good idea of what the final product of the conference committee will look like.

After the conference committee acts and sends the bill to the president, we will have a stronger section 201, one that will require or at least urge greater participation by the industry in thinking about the planning for its future. It is likely to be interpreted by most people as a very small movement down a very long path toward industrial policy.

18
Protectionism

Daniel Oliver

Congress is considering a wide range of protectionist legislative proposals. The last time Congress had this degree of fervor over protectionism it enacted the Smoot-Hawley Tariff Act. That legislation started a trade war and helped plunge the world into the Great Depression.

This panel is supposed to focus on the suggestion from certain quarters that "industrial adjustment" sponsored and supervised by government would help solve our country's perceived trade problem. A few weeks ago, when I was testifying before the Senate Finance Committee, Senator Bradley asked me what I thought was the most potent weapon we could use against the Japanese to solve the problem of our trade deficit with them. I told Senator Bradley that I would have to question his premise that our trade deficit with Japan is a problem. His response—polite though it was—was, "Don't."

Today, fortunately, I don't need a senator's indulgence to discuss our premises. We can greatly clarify the true nature of the current trade policy debate by asking the following question: Suppose the country had no trade deficit but that some of our industries—such as automobiles, steel, textiles, machine tools, and computer chips—were facing vigorous foreign competition. Would we still have calls to protect those industries? Would we still be worrying about competitiveness in those industries?

We would have calls to protect them. We would have calls for adjustment policies and all the calls that we have today.

What has happened in the national debate over trade is that the special interests representing industries affected by foreign competition have clothed the real political issue in rhetoric about competitiveness and the evil Japanese. In essence, the special interests have tried to hijack the debate. They have invented a national problem to advance their own special interests.

Protectionists do not seem to be embarrassed to use any argument, no matter how specious. A powerful proponent of protection-ism warns that American workers are becoming "hewers of wood and drawers of water." Drawers of water? Well, there is some truth in that. We have seen numerous American workers in Washington, D.C., carrying water for industries seeking government protection from competition.

Two major myths are advanced by the protectionists in the cur-rent debate. The first myth is that protectionism is justified by a trade deficit. The second myth is that protectionism saves jobs. Both are wrong.

A trade deficit—or a surplus for that matter, as any number of economists will tell you—is not something that is good or bad in itself.[1] Mexico, for example, runs a trade surplus, but do we want to copy Mexico's economy?

A nation's trade deficit, the so-called current account deficit, is merely the counterpart to its capital account surplus. During the 1970s the United States had a trade surplus and a deficit in the capital account, partly because of the large amounts of U.S. direct investment overseas. We are now running a surplus in our capital account be-cause the favorable climate for investment in the United States has caused an influx of foreign capital that has partially financed a major retooling of American production capacity. If the rest of the world is to invest on net in the United States, the United States will necessarily run a trade deficit.

The second major myth of protectionism is that it would save jobs. Sometimes we hear this myth in the form that trade deficits mean lost jobs. The economist Herbert Stein has characterized this myth as "best-selling fiction," since no other claim about trade deficits is so easily refuted. The United States, in the face of trade deficits, continues to produce new jobs at a rate envied by other developed countries. Of course, foreign competition may cost identifiable, politi-cally visible jobs in a particular industry. But it is also a fact—one conveniently not mentioned by the protectionists—that protectionist measures generally cost jobs in the economy as a whole. Unfortu-nately, those jobs are often not identifiable, and they tend not to be politically visible.

The jobs issue raised by the protectionists is specious. What we are really talking about is saving jobs in the steel industry or in the machine tool industry at the expense of jobs in manufacturing or saving jobs in computer chips at the expense of jobs in electronics and so on. If trade is restricted, jobs will be lost in the export sector when foreign countries find they have fewer dollars to spend on American products.[2] Where, for example, do the American dollars that Mexicans use to buy American products largely come from? When we place tariffs on imports, foreign countries make fewer sales here and so have fewer dollars with which to purchase American exports. If trade is restricted, jobs will also be lost in sectors that use imports whose prices are raised by restriction of imports. One example comes from last week's news about the current computer chip war. U.S. electronics and computer companies told us that they need to buy computer chips at world prices or they cannot compete in world markets.

Using government policy to take jobs away from some to protect the jobs of others is bad enough. What makes it worse is that protectionism is a very expensive way of saving jobs in a particular industry. Federal Trade Commission studies estimate that the annual cost to the economy for every job protected in industries such as steel and automobiles often exceeds $100,000 per year. So protecting steel not only takes away jobs in manufacturing but also forces consumers to subsidize those "saved" jobs at a rate of about five times the going wage.

To sum up, protectionism is not justified by a trade deficit, and protectionism does not save jobs. Trade restrictions will always be special-interest policy, the sacrifice of the general welfare for the benefit of a politically powerful minority.

Now we come to the question of adjustment. The real political issue in the adjustment debate is how to buy off the special interests at a smaller price than the cost that current protectionist proposals would impose on our economy, both in total jobs and in cost to consumers. Of course, Americans in some industries face displacement because of foreign competition. Perhaps it is appropriate for the government to give those people some help. In many cases, however, it already has—in the form of so-called voluntary restraint agreements that limit imports and save jobs in the protected industry. But helping people in trouble is not the only form of protectionism being advocated. The protectionists have managed to cloak their special-interest goals in the flag of competitiveness. They tell us we need to help industry not just to prevent human misery but so that we can beat the Japanese.

Most of the proposals being marketed as adjustment policies are "industrial policy" in its worst sense. Of course, the advocates of such policies prefer to ignore the long history of many countries' attempts to provide adjustment assistance to threatened industries, including our own experience during the New Deal. In many countries with active adjustment policies, it is difficult to close a factory or to replace a worker. If we make it more difficult to close or sell an inefficient factory, we can expect fewer factories to be built. If it becomes more expensive to hire a worker because of the minimum wage laws or more difficult to fire a worker, fewer workers will be hired.

The actual effect of adjustment policies, as of many government policies, is often the opposite of the intended effect. The reason in this case is clear. Many of the people in the industry given assistance do not want to adjust; they want to be protected. If the industry is powerful enough to get the adjustment assistance, it is usually powerful enough to resist adjustments, as long as taxpayers will pay the bill.

Of the current proposals, one in particular deserves comment. S. 490, Senator Bentsen's trade bill, would, in effect, change the so-called escape clause, section 201 of the Trade Act of 1974, into an industry collusion statute. The government would provide not only a sanctioned forum for reaching an agreement and a degree of antitrust immunity but government monitoring to police the agreement as well. If this sort of central planning is what adjustment means, we want no part of it.

The United States continues to produce new jobs because our economy is dynamic. A dynamic economy that is allowed to adjust to changes in prices, incomes, and technology will produce new firms, new products, and new jobs. Forty years ago the economist Joseph Schumpeter described the capitalist engine of growth as a process of creative destruction. He argued that this machine for improving the living standard of everyone is durable and self-sustaining, but he warned that it could be destroyed "with sufficient help from the public sector." This will surely happen if the government bows to special interests and protects them from competition. That is the lesson of the Smoot-Hawley Act.

Hewers of wood and drawers of water? Yes, indeed. If the current protectionists had been around in the sixteenth century, they would have been introducing legislation to protect the federated woodsmen from coal imports.

History shows that economies not allowed to adjust will become stagnant; economies not allowed to contract in one sector will not expand in other sectors. The special interests' so-called adjustment policies must be exposed for what they are: policies that will benefit particular interests at a cost of undermining our competitiveness. Competitiveness means making our products more competitive in world markets. No policy will be more successful at this than the policy of free trade.

Notes

1. See Herbert Stein, "Leave the Trade Deficit Alone," *Wall Street Journal*, March 11, 1987; Milton Friedman and Rose Friedman, *Free to Choose* (1980); "Trade Deficit Bogeyman," *Wall Street Journal*, September 13, 1985; and Alan Reynolds, " 'Mainstream Economics': None Dare Call it Voodoo," *Wall Street Journal*, May 7, 1984.

2. See Kenneth W. Clements and Larry A. Sjaastad, "How Protection Taxes Exporters" (Trade Policy Research Center, 1984).

19

The Importance of Process

Alan Wolff

I find myself completely in opposition to the statements made by Chairman Oliver. I see a different world out there from the one he sees. I do not see the House or the Senate engaged in rampant protectionism. I do not think that Jack Danforth or Lloyd Bentsen or Dan Rostenkowski or Bill Frenzel or Sam Gibbons or Don Pease is engaged in legislating protectionism. And I do not think that is what the result of the bill is going to be.

I find it very strange to be here as a defender of Reagan administration trade policy, and I won't defend all of it by any means. But since I represent the semiconductor industry, I have to acknowledge that the actions of the administration are far from anything that should be labeled protectionist. We should not, in defense of free trade, allow any foreign government's excess, any rampant Japanese mercantilism, to define the shape of the United States economy— which is what would have happened if the Japanese had been allowed to continue to exclude us from their market while selling chips year in and year out at below the cost of production. Last year the Japanese producers lost $2 billion on selling chips. Faced with this kind of competition for long, our people would go out of business. Some would say that might be an advantage for consumers. But the consumers of chips—the computer companies—are largely in favor of this agreement and have been strong backers of it. They fear dependence on their vertically integrated competitors.

Turning to the debate on the Hill, on 201, the escape clause, it is not, by and large, a debate over protectionism. The question is not whether to restrict imports but whether, if imports are restricted a better job can be done than is currently being done and has been done under existing law. There is broad agreement among both Republicans and Democrats in the House and the Senate that a better job can be done, substantially along the lines that Representative Pease outlined.

There is a pretense of nonintervention that gets people into a lot of trouble. This country's government has intervened in steel trade for twenty years. It pretends that it does not, but it intervenes very extensively in the automobile trade. The question is, What do we as a nation get out of that process? As far as anyone can tell, pure protection without any analysis or understanding of whether we are getting value for the taxpayers, for all of us as consumers.

I am counsel to a group called the Labor Industry Coalition for International Trade. It consists of a number of major American companies, with very diverse trade philosophies, and the industrial unions of the AFL-CIO. It includes major exporters; it also includes companies that are somewhat defensive about imports in their area. We do not take sectoral positions. We do take positions on trade law reform.

The provisions in the House bill stem in part from ideas that the steelworkers originated. The steelworkers have been the so-called beneficiaries of years of voluntary restraint in the late 1960s and early 1970s, over several administrations. Finally, this administration came in; it was doctrinarily of the view that free trade was the policy of the hour. It allowed the trigger price mechanism—a protective device to prevent foreign subsidized goods and dumped goods from eroding our industry too quickly—to lapse.

What was the result? Now global quotas have been put into place. In the name of free trade we have backed into a system of complete controls. Those quotas are not auctioned. There is no revenue to the Treasury. And the question of adjustment has not been effectively addressed at all.

Again the issue is not whether to impose restrictions. That will happen in any event under United States law. It is a wise law, because if the government does not intervene when there is serious injury from imports to allow some period for adjustment, support for an open trading system will erode, and our borders will ultimately close. That is the lesson in steel, a lesson we should learn because unadulterated, unthinking protection has a tendency to spread.

What would the current proposals seek to do? They would seek to do a better job of imposing restrictions. There should be an adjustment plan put forward, bringing industry together with labor and government, when a major import relief case is considered. It should be optional. Not every industry will be able to formulate such a plan (a requirement in the Senate bill). Should it involve labor and industry and government in one forum? I think it should.

Why? For example, no labor union is politically in the position of being able simply to say, "You're right. Part of our problem of compet-

itiveness or erosion of productivity is high wages and work rules."
That conclusion can only emerge as part of a bargaining process.
There has to be a process in which a labor leader can come out of the
room and say, "Well, this is what we have to do, guys, but let me tell
you what we got. We got three years of relief." Right now the
government simply grants the relief.

The firms have some vision of what is necessary. I represented
several steel companies for several years. Their vice-presidents for
corporate development are not unaware of what it takes to make steel
competitively. They are unable to finance their plans, however—
whether continuous costing for integrated mills or minimills or any
form of major modernization. They simply cannot go to the market.
They cannot go to the banks—they do not know how long relief will
last. There is no process by which steel or some other industries can
be effectively rationalized.

Who will evaluate that plan? It should be someone who has the
power to grant relief. It should be the U.S. trade representative, who
can go to the rest of the government because it is always a consultative
process. I strongly support the transfer of authority to the U.S. trade
representative. He should be able to justify to the rest of the government that he is getting something in return for the overall national
interest, that is, a more competitive industry.

There should be discretion in whether to impose restrictions,
however. The Senate bill currently provides that if the International
Trade Commission is unanimous, relief must be granted. I think that
is an error.

Causation is another issue before the Congress. The problem is
this: In a recession industries that experience a great deal of cyclical
demand will never be able to get relief because recession will always
be the largest cause of their import problem. They cannot get relief on
the high side of the business cycle because they are showing some
profits, though not enough to carry them through the low end. So
they are out of luck at all times.

On the Pease proposal, I do not think industry can very successfully sit down with labor and come up with an overall scheme. The
word "plan" overstates what is feasible. Industries can identify problems and some possible solutions. Some of these will be public policy
solutions. They may involve changes in tax policy. They may involve
changes in environmental regulation, which is what occurred in steel
in the late 1970s.

What is needed is a bottom-up, not a top-down, approach, where
the individual companies say, "This is what we can do. If you allow us
some antitrust relief to combine part of our facilities in the following

way with some of our competitors, we might do a better job of things. If I knew I had five years of relief, this is the kind of automation I would put into place. This is what my workers will be willing to do with respect to wages." Labor does have to make a contribution as a precondition for relief if it can.

But the granting of relief should not be mandatory. The executive needs some flexibility in dealing with these problems.

The International Trade Commission, for example, mandated relief in the case of copper. The administration and the cabinet were unanimous in opposing relief because it could not have improved the ore grade of copper in this country. It was a fundamental competitive problem that import restrictions would not have cured, *and* the downstream industries would have been gravely injured.

In sum, process is very important. This administration, which has been afraid of being labeled as engaging in anything resembling industrial policy, has nevertheless engaged heavily in industrial policy but with the single tool of import restrictions. That is pure protectionism, unleavened in any way by gains in adjustment or increased competitiveness.

20
Making Relief Conditional on Adjustment

Paul C. Rosenthal

I ought to identify whom I have represented in the past, just to get things straight. My firm represents the specialty steel industry and represented the steelworkers and Bethlehem Steel in the escape clause case that brought the voluntary restraint agreements.

It is interesting hearing the debate about industrial policy, which used to be the buzzword. Mr. Mondale ran on a platform that stressed an industrial policy component. That term disappeared after the 1984 election. Then the new buzzword was competitive policy. In writing this article I contemplated just taking out the word "industrial", from an earlier article wherever it appeared in the word processor and substituting the word "competitive" to bring it up to date that way.

The Reagan administration's approach in its new competitive policy bill is very interesting. One of the fascinating things to me during the escape clause processes was the administration's absolute abhorrence of anything that could be labeled an industrial policy. Yet the administration was willing to grant some form of relief. On the other side the United Steelworkers very much wanted a conditional relief, wanted to make sure that if relief were granted the steel companies would use the period of relief to reinvest and to modernize.

The administration decided to have voluntary restraint agreements on steel. It was left to Congress—at the steelworkers' urging—to require in the Steel Import Stabilization Act the reinvestment of any cash flow derived from the import relief period for modernization. As a condition of that relief, the International Trade Commission and the U.S. trade representative were required to monitor whether all the cash flow of the major companies was reinvested in the industry, as opposed, for example, to buying oil companies.

The problem is not the bogeyman of protectionism or of special interests. There has been an escape clause in our law as there has been an escape clause in the laws of virtually all our trading partners, ever since the GATT came into being. We and our trading partners have recognized that at some point an industry may need relief from serious injury caused by import competition. The only question has been under what conditions relief is granted.

Representative Pease quite rightly points out that there has been dissatisfaction with granting relief and doing nothing more—nothing to see whether relief is being effectively used and whether the people who have got the relief will be able to stop asking for it after the relief period ends. The big problem that Congress has been facing is how to ensure adjustment once import relief is granted. How does one make sure that the import relief granted is designed to aid in that adjustment?

The idea of an adjustment plan is a very good one. Every industry asking for relief ought to be able to say, This is what we plan to do during the relief period. But we should be very cautious about what to expect from such an adjustment plan. A lot will depend on the size of the industry. Whether it is a one-company industry like motorcycles or a hundred-company industry like steel or footwear makes a tremendous difference to how useful an adjustment plan will be.

The nature of the industry also makes a difference. If it includes both large and small companies, it will be hard to reach agreement on how adjustments should be made.

I agree with Chairman Oliver about the antitrust collusion aspects of these adjustment plans. It would be very difficult to have an adjustment plan that really does something and at the same time does not skirt the antitrust laws. I expect that the adjustment plans that are or should be presented will be very general and will allow companies and unions within the industry individually to suggest precisely what they plan to do during an import relief period.

The House took very sensible action in scaling down what would be required in an adjustment plan or who would do it. The tripartite idea sounds great in theory, but it is impossible to have industry, labor, and government agree on anything within 120 days, as the original House proposal called for. Having seen tripartite efforts in steel try to develop a plan to aid the steel industry, I am very pessimistic about doing anything in that short a time.

Having said all that, I do think it is necessary to go through the effort. The people who are paying for relief—inevitably it is paid for by consumers, by the society as a whole—must have some assurance that when the period is over, a more efficient industry will survive.

21

The Politics of
Industrial Adjustment

Claude E. Barfield, Daniel Oliver, and Don J. Pease

MR. BARFIELD: It seems that both sides of this issue have a difficult puzzle. In talking about section 201, we are not just talking about industrial policies starting from a clean slate. The opponents have to answer the question that Paul Rosenthal raised. In 201 as it has been structured for relief, the private sector has approached the government for the use of public resources. There are costs involved in changing environmental legislation or tax policy or whatever. How does one then oppose getting a reasonable return on those public resources? That is the side, it seems to me, that is a puzzle for the opponents.

On the other side how do you ensure—as Adam Smith said several centuries ago—that when two or three businessmen get together even to drink tea, you don't have a conspiracy against the public interest? Without a conspiracy against the public interest, it is hard to believe that rational plans would come out. In other words, we are caught between those two conundrums.

MR. PEASE: I don't agree or disagree with much of what has been said. Dan Oliver has laid out the classic, theoretical free trade position, and there is a lot of truth to it. I think the rest of us would argue that you cannot follow anything precisely in theory. We are practical people, we deal in the real world, and while operating within a framework of free trade, we have to try to do some things that seem to make sense and do not violate the basic principles.

What the free traders have to keep in mind is that the private sector will approach the government for relief. The political pressure will be there—pressure from the companies that are facing competition overseas; loss of sales; pressure from the workers; and pressure from the communities. No politician wants to go back home to a town that has just lost its only or primary source of employment and trumpet the gospel of free trade. That is not a satisfactory response.

The questions are: Are we going to have an ad hoc response to pressures like that? Are we going to wait until the steel industry comes in and then deal with the trigger price mechanism? Are we going to wait for the auto industry to come in and have voluntary restraints? Are we going to wait for the machine tool industry to come in? Will we decide on an ad hoc basis in each case what relief to provide? Or are we going to try to have a structure that in a sense insulates the politicians among us, the members of Congress, from the pressure of having to "do something" right away? It is very useful to be able to say: I am very sympathetic, you have lost your job, the plant has closed, but we have a mechanism for dealing with that. That mechanism is in place and it is working. Let's give it six months or a year and see how it plays out.

Second, are we going to get anything for the relief that we give? That has been a theme of this entire discussion this afternoon. What Congress is considering doing in section 201 is strengthening the structure so that we can give a more satisfactory answer to our constituents and try to build in a quid pro quo. That is eminently good policy.

MR. OLIVER: The jobs produced by the system we have now indicate quite clearly that the country as a whole is doing very well, notwithstanding the trade deficit, even if some industries are being battered by competition. People talk in terms of destructive competition, but destructive competition means that consumers have voted with their dollars to choose product A or producer A over producer B. Destructive competition is really the result of consumer choice. It seems to have worked quite well, and I would not be in favor of abandoning free trade because of problems in a particular industry.

I understand that there is a political problem for congressmen. Anybody who holds an elected position has to go back to the district and talk to people who may have been displaced by foreign competition. But, of course, there are also people who have been displaced by domestic competition. It doesn't seem to me that people displaced by foreign competition should get better treatment than any worker displaced by domestic competition. That surely is treating one's constituents unequally, and none of us would want that to happen. It seems to me that Congress's most appropriate response to people who think they need some special relief is to adopt Mrs. Reagan's solution, "Just Say No," or, if you prefer, "Just Say No, Thank You."

I get the impression that Representative Pease is saying that we have to engage in a charade. We have to have a formula and a process that people can go through, so that they will think that they are getting relief, whereas in the end they won't.

My answer to that is that the thing to do is to talk about the benefits of free trade, talk about the benefits of the free market, tell the community what free trade has produced, talk about the increase in jobs, and remind people that jobs and industries change. There is a process of creative destruction, and we want to make sure there are jobs around for their children as well as for them. The free market approach that we have been using for the past six years and the statistics that practice has demonstrated clearly indicate that free trade is the way to create jobs and to maximize our consumer welfare. If we all talk about that, even the people who are temporarily hurt by dislocating practices will begin to understand the benefits of the free market.

MR. PEASE: A quick intervention here, in case there happen to be any reporters from the *Norwalk Reflector* or the *Ashland Times-Gazette* or other newspapers in my district. I don't intend to engage in a charade at all. Politicians like myself need to have something to talk about when we go back home. I want to say to the workers, yes, we will help you get retrained, and to the communities, yes, we will help you through the Economic Development Administration and other agencies to find new tenants for the factories that have become vacant. I think it serves a political purpose to have something to talk about, but I want some substance behind the statement.

MR. OLIVER: The prosecution rests.

Part Seven

Labor Adjustment:
Aid or Barrier to Competitiveness?

22

More Options for
the Displaced Worker

Malcolm R. Lovell, Jr.

Is labor adjustment an aid or a barrier to competitiveness? I think it is vital to competitiveness—whether it is an aid or a barrier is a question of how it is done. It can be very disruptive to economic change, or it can be very supportive of economic change.

In general, I see societies coping with labor adjustment in three different ways. In Europe, for a number of years the labor adjustment has determined the speed of the economic adjustment. In many instances, Europeans have striven to protect existing jobs and to get employment security in that fashion, rather than to help an individual move to new work. This approach often discourages change in threatened industries.

In Japan, a coalition of government and industry often helps arrange for workers to move—at least in large industries—from work that is no longer needed or no longer competitive to work that is needed more. That does not happen for everybody in Japan, obviously, but for those employed in the large corporations.

In the United States, what we have always done, and what I imagine we will continue to do, is to rely on the individual displaced worker to assume the basic responsibility to find new work, and to provide a wide variety of options, both public and private, to help that process work better. Our task force decided that the options up to now did not represent an adequate range to do a responsible job in helping the adjustment take place.

We agreed that change was a necessary part of an adjustment process as a society struggles to maintain a high standard of living and maintain itself at the forefront of international competitiveness. Although nobody on the task force was really arguing that change should be restricted or discouraged, we believed that we had to provide this wider variety of options for the individuals who were displaced through no fault of their own.

What we recommended, I think, has a very good chance to be enacted into law. As most are aware, the president has recommended a billion dollars in the budget for this purpose, and legislation now on Capitol Hill would carry out many of our recommendations. A number of bills in both the House and the Senate address the question and allocate funds to provide labor market information, training, and various other adjustment assistance to workers in need.

Two areas are the focus of quite a bit of disagreement and conflict, however. The first, and probably the most vexing, is the question of mandatory notice on plant closings. The task force was unanimous in saying that notice was a very important and helpful piece of information to have to help workers move to new jobs. There was no argument about the usefulness of it, particularly when it was associated with sensitive actions taken to meet the needs of the individual faced with a move. The only disagreement was whether that notice should be mandatory. I am hopeful that some sort of understanding can be worked out between the business and the labor community that would be satisfactory to Congress. Whether that is possible is not clear, but if so, that is a better way to proceed.

The other issue in conflict is the delivery mechanism of public services to displaced workers. The task force felt that it was important that somebody be held responsible for making the program work and decided that in all likelihood the governor of the state in question was the logical candidate for that responsibility. So often a public policy is designed to meet certain political considerations, and questions of effectiveness often take second place to more expedient considerations. Then everybody is surprised when the program does not work as well as it was hoped.

A basic management concept is to give responsibility to somebody for carrying out the objectives that are set out. Congress should set the goals to help individuals move quickly to new work, allocate the resources, and then provide money to the states through the governors. The federal government could then carefully monitor what is happening, evaluate it, and provide technical assistance. Afterwards, the successes of those governors that do well can be made public, and the governors can bask in the glory; and those that do poorly would have to stand up and be counted and try to do better. In all probability, some states will do better than others, and if they set good examples and develop systems that work better than others, they can be emulated.

It is very important to make it clear who is responsible for the success and not tie their hands. Some of the other provisions that have been suggested specify that other institutions, such as the service delivery areas and the private industry councils, should have special roles.

Those are the two main questions yet to be resolved. Of course, there's always the problem of legislation of this sort, with a lot of bipartisan support, becoming confused with legislation without such support, and the whole effort is lost. I used to fear that more than I do today. I am moderately optimistic that there is a broad recognition in the country that we should deal sensitively with the needs of displaced workers as we struggle to maintain a high level of competitiveness and a high standard of living, that these roughly 1 million individuals a year that we have been displacing will not bear an undue burden; and that we make proper private and public efforts to move them quickly to other work.

23

The Urgency of Assistance to Displaced Workers

Jay Rockefeller

I agree with Mr. Lovell that there will be a bill. I frankly think there is very little chance of failure, and I hope the bill will be bipartisan. There will be some bumps along the way—I am hopeful, however, that a solid piece of legislation develops and is enacted soon to expand, speed up, and strengthen the federal role in worker adjustment. I say that from my experience first as governor and now as senator of the state that leads the nation—I'm sorry to say—not only in the rate of plant closings but in proportions of dislocated workers.

That's not a very happy circumstance. It's also not a very new circumstance for central Appalachia. For counties with over 40 percent unemployment, we look for ways to do something about it. We have had major wholesale manufacturing move out of the state—as in the case of Volkswagen's move to Mexico—and a lot of other very painful plant closings and dislocations.

Our problem is not just a question of imports, although our percentage of jobs lost to imports is now a much bigger percentage of GNP than it once was, up from about 4 to about 11 percent. It is not just imports that cause these jobs to move but also dislocation and other economic so-called adjustments. We cannot think of this dislocation as a temporary affair, either: our economy is in fundamental readjustment; we all know that. So is the rest of the world's; they all know that. A million jobs a year are being lost in the United States. In a recent five-year span, half those who found new jobs had to take a cut in pay. Of the 11 million workers who lost their jobs during these years, 5 million had worked three years or more at their former job; those who eventually found jobs were out of work an average of twenty-seven weeks, almost seven months.

We have this very strange system in our country now that when somebody is out of work, the state and the federal government do precious little to help them. In fact, statistics show that even with state and federal efforts combined, only about 5 percent of the jobless will receive help. Unlike any other industrialized country that I know of, the United States ignores 95 percent of those who are out of work as a result of imports or economic dislocation. We simply don't attend to them.

At a time when everybody is talking about trying to compete with the Japanese now and with the Brazilians and others in another decade or so, that kind of human resource waste makes no sense. It is not just a matter of compassion, although that is part of it. Sometimes people who have worked at an aluminum plant or a steel plant or a coal mine, operating extremely efficiently, are all of a sudden out of work, on the street, with nowhere to go. Often their communities have no other kind of work available. These workers used to be able, as they were frequently told, to go to Houston, but now there is no work in Houston either. There is nothing for them to do.

Ignoring the 95 percent is bad enough, but even many of those that we do help cannot get that help, sometimes until many months have passed. Let me give an example to show the fundamental problem in our present policy.

About 1,000 coal miners in West Virginia were laid off in June 1986 and could make a case that the cause was imports since the mine that shut down was owned by USX Steel. When USX Steel failed because of so-called steel dumping, it shut mines including this one in southern West Virginia. The problem was that the laid-off miners were not aware of the fact that they could apply and qualify for "Trade Adjustment Assistance," the federal program specifically charged with helping "import-injured" workers to readjust through retraining and other services. When they did learn about TAA, they applied for assistance in late July or so and were not certified for assistance by the secretary of labor until January 1987. And by the time they signed up for training, seven or eight months after being laid off, there was no money left—Congress had not appropriated enough.

Although they received fifty-two weeks of weekly income assistance payments after their twenty-six weeks of unemployment insurance, they could get no training. What happens to somebody—a coal miner out of work or a steelworker or an auto worker or a chemical worker or a glass worker—after four or five months? The point is we must have "rapid response" to dislocated workers, and that is what some of these bills are trying to provide, similar to the Canadian model, the Japanese model, and the West German model. But let's consider just the Canadian model.

In Canada labor and management work together when they

101

know that a plant or a mine is going to close, and they both prepare for it. Within a week after the closing of the plant, state or federal teams are on the spot working with labor and management to help people begin the transition.

John Heinz of Pennsylvania and I have introduced such a bill. We've had some hearings, one in Pittsburgh, for example, for which a number of people came up from my state. One fellow epitomized the problem. He was a very skilled worker who had worked for a long time at Volkswagen, a stamping plant in South Charleston, West Virginia; he was twenty-seven years old, with a wife and family, and he was laid off. Then he was pulled back to work for a while and laid off again. Now he wants to be a computer technician, but it takes a year to learn that skill. A person cannot switch from even the sophisticated job of operating a stamping machine to the job of repairing computers without a year of training. His problem was not import related; his company moved to Mexico.

Unfortunately, 20 percent of the displaced workers in our country are functionally illiterate, which means that they must learn basic skills: math, reading, communications.

Any bill worth its salt in Congress today must cover those basic skills and provide the money to pay for their acquisition. Moreover, the money must last long enough, not only to teach the basic skills but also to provide the training and job search assistance. It takes about a year for a person to retool his or her skills with the income to pay for that training.

I hope that we will make the money available to give people sufficient training and to sustain them financially long enough so that they can get it. In addition, I'm hoping that we will build a rapid response system. Our industries, in fact, have not been very good at telling workers when plants are going to close down or at giving any warning. That makes it very difficult for anybody to plan. Rapid response, Canadian-style, is necessary.

I have a great deal of respect for Secretary Brock, the task force, and what they have done. Everybody knows what the answers are. The question now is to get a bill through Congress with bipartisan support and enough money. The money proposed by both Republicans and Democrats is probably not sufficient to do the entire job, but it should get us headed in the right direction.

In conclusion, I think it's silly to have two different programs, a Trade Adjustment Assistance and Title III, the Dislocated Workers Assistance Program under the Job Training Partnership Act. I'm not going to fight trying to join those programs because I understand perfectly well that if TAA is merged into the other program we lose the more generous benefits that TAA provides to import-injured workers. The confusion and frustration of trying to deal with one agency for TAA and an entirely separate agency for Title III—neither of them with any idea what the other is doing—are boundless.

If we can coordinate our efforts to provide basic skills, enough income to give people time to acquire training for jobs that do exist, and rapid response, we will have ourselves a better country.

24
Myths Surrounding Displaced Workers

Howard D. Samuel

I have worked for many years in the labor movement, most of the time with a union serving the industry in which more companies have gone out of business or been more severely affected by international trade than any other—the apparel industry. During those years, I also spent three years in the Labor Department in charge of the Bureau of International Labor Affairs, which included the responsibility for enforcing the Trade Adjustment Assistance program. So I speak with a little experience there, not all terribly happy either.

I want to address some myths about this whole issue. Myth number one had to do with Trade Adjustment Assistance. Some people still believe that Trade Adjustment Assistance was put in the trade bill to help workers adjust to the impact of international trade. Of course, nothing could be farther from the truth. TAA is not an adjustment program; it's a compensation program. In my union, when some of our members first took advantage of it, the last thing we wanted them to do was to adjust out of our industry. At that time we could not foresee what would happen. We wanted some kind of compensation during the six to eight or ten months that they were out of work, so that when they came back to work they could come back reasonably whole, with more support than simply unemployment insurance, which, of course, lasts only six months.

TAA does serve that purpose then. Why was it in the bill in the first place? I think all of us are fully aware why: we probably would not have had a trade bill without Trade Adjustment Assistance. Trade Adjustment Assistance helps Congress and the administration sell and open trading policy. So there is a real political importance to Trade Adjustment Assistance, and there is some importance in compensation. But is it what we should do for our workers? That's the question, and I think Senator Rockefeller advanced that question very well.

As for myth number one, then, TAA it is not an adjustment program: it is a compensation program, and it can get very expensive. In an administration that was far more tight-fisted than this administration, we were spending almost $2 billion by 1980 in Trade Adjustment Assistance, higher than it is now.

Myth number two is that dislocated workers are really just a bunch of high-paid (behind the scenes people say overpaid) auto and steel workers, and we do not have to shed great crocodile tears for them. They have been making it for years, and now finally it's caught up to them. Right? In fact, a majority of displaced workers earn less than the average manufacturing wage. There are auto and steel workers and some miners, but there are far more shoe workers and hat workers and apparel workers and textile workers.

Myth number three is that this problem is strictly regional. Why should the nation get upset when displacement affects only the few so-called Rust Belt states in the middle of the country? Wrong. The highest dislocation rates are in the South and in the mountain states. There are a lot of displaced workers in the Rust Belt, of course, because there are a lot of workers in the Rust Belt. But the highest rate is not in the Rust Belt.

Myth number four is that advance notice is really a moral issue. It is only fair that we notify workers before they are about to lose their jobs, through either a mass layoff or a closed plant. It is only fair that we inform the community. Of course, it is only fair, but the real reason why those of us in the labor movement and our friends in Congress favor making advance notice mandatory is that it is the only way we can ensure an adequate adjustment process. It is the best way, and sometimes the only way, to get a worker's mind turned toward adjustment. Once that worker has left the plant gate for the last time, he begins to think of himself as a jobless worker with no place to go. He is subject to loss of morale or self-confidence or to possible family problems, health problems, alcoholism, drugs, even suicide. Weeks beforehand the worker must begin operating in a new mode, looking for new work, changing his skills, or improving his literacy and the like, long before he walks out the last time, long before he becomes, in effect, unemployed.

Myth number five is that most workers are now getting advance notice; why are we becoming so upset? In fact, most workers do not get advance notice. About two-thirds of blue-collar workers get advance notice of two weeks or less. The average notice period for nonunion blue collar workers is just *two* days. Most workers do not get adequate advance notice; many workers get none whatsoever.

Myth number six holds that things are getting better; perhaps in the past no one got advance notice but now with all the publicity, increased plant closings and mass layoffs, and the greater understanding of plant managers, more workers are getting it. Not so. The fact is that Bureau of Labor Statistics data show the incidence of advance notice did not improve from 1984 to 1986. The situation is not getting any better whatsoever. Most workers still get no warning.

Moreover, some people assume that the larger companies, those employing more than 500 people, give advance notice and that our problem is not with them, but with the little companies, those in my industry, the apparel industry, for example. There is in fact no difference whatsoever in the incidence of advance notice between companies that employ more than 500 and companies that employ fewer than 500. Workers today in America are not being given advance notice to nearly the extent they should be. Advance notice is the exception, not the rule. Correcting this situation is long overdue; these workers must come back into the labor force as quickly as possible because the longer they are out, the more costly it is for you and me as taxpayers. These people deserve better from our country.

25

Labor Adjustment, Retraining, and Advance Notice of Closings

Marvin H. Kosters

Whatever might be said about our economy, the labor market has performed remarkably well in recent years throughout the period of recession, deregulation, and significant foreign trade competition. There have, of course, been some difficulties. The most serious problems have been the result of big layoffs in relatively small communities with small labor markets. Some of Senator Rockefeller's counties might qualify in that regard, for example.

In fact, however, the big share of workers displaced by plant closings and mass layoffs have gotten jobs quite quickly. They have gotten jobs at wages that are sometimes lower initially but that compare reasonably favorably with their previous wages, even though they have just started on these new jobs. We need to keep the problem in perspective.

As for what to do about the very small fraction of unemployed with serious problems, I find merit in the notion of setting up some sort of displaced workers' unit with specific responsibility, as Mr. Lovell suggested earlier. I also agree with Senator Rockefeller that consolidating our programs, particularly Trade Adjustment Assistance and the other programs intended to remedy matters, is a good idea. In much of the present discussion, however, there is more emphasis on training than I would prefer to see for this group of workers. It is very awkward to speak against training, of course, and I agree that training can be very valuable. The question is, really, whether training is a good investment for most of these experienced workers. The number of displaced workers who do not get a job quickly and who could benefit from training is probably much smaller than is suggested in many of the current spending proposals.

On the question of mandatory advance notice, there is a great deal of confusion. I will present some numbers that are quite different from those that Howard Samuel presented, for example. It is true that *specific* advance notice—informing each individual worker about the precise date when their jobs will terminate—frequently occurs without long lead time. When *general* advance notice is considered, however—an announcement that a General Motors plant is scheduled to close in six months, for example—a much larger fraction of workers get advance notice and lead times are much longer.

According to the GAO report, some 80 percent of firms give general advance notice. When both general and specific notice are considered together, the fraction of firms that give advance notice rises to 88 percent with almost 60 percent giving more than two weeks' lead time. General notice may be the most important for workers because it is the main way in which they are alerted so they can take advantage of opportunities that come their way or avoid making decisions that they would later regret when the plant is closed.

It is generally agreed by almost everyone concerned that providing advance notice is a good idea. It is also agreed that there need to be exceptions. Many times advance notice is simply not feasible, certainly not three to six months ahead of time as the bills require. Consequently, we need a variety of kinds of exceptions. My concern about mandatory advance notice requirements is that very few benefits would accrue. It is entirely possible that most firms that do not now give general advance notice are unable to do so, and that most would qualify under the exception process. If so, we would obtain few benefits, but we would incur significant costs. Employment adjustments would become much more costly to firms. They would need to adjust in other ways, such as avoiding the hiring of additional workers and relying instead on more overtime. They would need to carry larger inventories, which would add to business costs. In summary, we could get a bill imposing mandatory advance notice requirements that would bring us many costs but very few benefits.

26

Balancing Competitiveness with Assistance to Workers

*Marvin L. Esch, Marvin H. Kosters, Malcolm R. Lovell, Jr.,
Jay Rockefeller, and Howard D. Samuel*

MR. ESCH: Mr. Samuel, you suggested that, in fact, the current trade adjustment program is an additional compensation program rather than a true adjustment program. You were also very open in suggesting that the difficulty in adjustment programs is that the individual may move out of that employment sector, indeed out of that union. What type of adjustment program, other than the basic compensation and carryover program to provide basic needs, do you recommend? Is there another model we should look at?

MR. SAMUEL: The reason that the TAA could not serve as an adjustment model is that there is a lag between the time the worker leaves the plant and the time he receives his benefits. That lag occurs because the government has to certify that a worker really lost his or her job because of the impact of imports.

MR. ESCH: Is there any way to expedite that process?

MR. SAMUEL: When I began my stint with the goverment in 1977, that screening took up to fourteen months. That is, the average worker received a check fourteen months after he or she left the job. We worked like the devil and got it down to nine, and I presume it could probably come down a bit from that, but not much because the average worker does not even submit the information to start the process until he has been unemployed seven months.

MR. ESCH: Do people understand it is a collective process?

MR. SAMUEL: Yes, that's right. TAA is not capable of being the kind of

109

program that we would like to see—which has to start with a rapid response long before the worker loses a job—with a panoply of government services, job search counseling, labor market information, training or retraining perhaps, remediation, and so forth.

MR. ESCH: What role do you see for the labor unions in that adjustment process?

MR. SAMUEL: We already play a role. As you are probably aware, the Human Resources Development Institute (HRDI) is an AFL-CIO institution that now receives funds from the government to provide training. A number of companies in the private sector offer programs jointly with unions. In the automobile industry, the communications industry, and elsewhere, there are some programs with labor and business together providing training programs and remediation for workers who lose their jobs.

Generally, I think labor should have some oversight authority to make sure that a government program operates properly, with the security of the worker in mind.

MR. ESCH: Senator Rockefeller, you've had a lot of experience in this area as the chief executive officer of West Virginia. How do you relate labor market adjustment to job creation?

Most governors today emphasize job creation within their own state. How does that need for job creation relate to the question of competitiveness?

MR. ROCKEFELLER: We face a classic dilemma. We must decide whether we are a regional, national, or international economy.

Fundamentally, what any governor wants is to have a job bank so that if someone is thrown out of work in a coal mine, for example, he can look for something else to do nearby. So then the question comes in this case, Does it have to be in West Virginia? Ultimately, for our national competitiveness, a worker in a state must receive the best possible training that he can, for what we hope might be available in that state. But if that work is not available, frankly, the objective is to get that person trained for a job somewhere.

MR. ESCH: Would you accept the need to encourage rather than discourage mobility of our workers?

MR. ROCKEFELLER: I don't think we encourage it as a matter of public policy, but it's happening as a matter of market policy. In rural states, often the largest employer in a county is the board of education, which is not national policy but local politics. The point is that we have a national economy, national marketplace. Frankly, I want to see the fellow from Volkswagen be a computer technician in West Virginia. If he has to go to Ohio or Detroit or California, however, it is more important to me that that person and his family hold together and have a job somewhere, even if we in West Virginia share his retraining with the state government that helped him get that training.

MR. KOSTERS: We have tried mobility programs for particular workers. In most instances, they have not worked very well, with good cause. That is, those people who lose a job for a specific reason are not necessarily the workers most likely to move out of the community. It may well be that somebody else moves and that the person who lost his job because of a plant closing takes a job made available in that way.

Of course, I think mobility is a very good idea, but that does not mean that we necessarily ought to subsidize mobility for any particular group. Moreover, I can see the attraction for someone from West Virginia—which, after all, is almost heaven, as advertised—to try to attract industry rather than to encourage its workers to move out.

MR. LOVELL: We are probably the most mobile nation in the world. That is one of our strengths. I do not think that workers in any other nation move as rapidly and as successfully as they do in the United States.

I believe that public policy should recognize that these moves do take place and that goverment should be supportive. I recognize the difficulties of encouraging someone to move or of paying a large part of the costs of a move. But to be supportive of a move and to recognize that it will take place, are I think, very useful.

MR. ROCKEFELLER: Everything becomes ideological when we discuss an area like worker readjustment: will it cost a lot of money, and what do the Republicans (or Democrats) think?

If we are trying to compete globally and we see the Japanese and the Koreans coming up in the apparel industry, for example, with Bangladesh and Brazil behind them, what are we doing to help displaced workers readjust for the country's future? It is not a question of who wins, labor or management, on a given issue.

If we cannot take people of ability and experience who are displaced from work (a million people a year) and do no better than retrain 5 percent of them to become productive parts of society, that is a national disgrace. There should not be ideological arguments about it. The question is, What works best to get a worker with the basic skills and the training and the knowledge and the confidence and the mobility, if necessary, so that he helps America grow, that he's at work and productive?

MR. ESCH: Are you satisfied that the task force presented adequate strategies to mobilize the resources of private industry, labor unions, community services, and education systems to focus on the question and synthesize those efforts? And should that impetus come from federal legislation, or should it come from a cooperative effort of those resources?

MR. ROCKEFELLER: Any time Kennedy, Metzenbaum, and Simon sign on to a report of a task force that is also endorsed by President Reagan, there must be something right. Yes, I think action has to be federal; I think the climate is clearly right for it. Frankly, I foresee an argument over plant closing notification, but the rest of it will sail through Congress.

MR. KOSTERS: I do not oppose training, but I do think that the real need for it must be put in perspective. The Bureau of Labor Statistics figures show a million or so workers on average displaced each year. In the first place, I think that number has recently been unusually high because of the recession. But we ought to ask ourselves what kind of workers these are and if they do need training.

Let me cite some percentages: 16 percent of the displaced workers are in managerial and professional occupations; 12.5 percent are sixty years old or over. Maybe these older workers should be retrained, but should we train workers in that age bracket at goverment expense? Twenty-eight percent were unemployed for five weeks or less, half the period of unemployment for the average unemployed worker; 9 percent are construction workers whose jobs terminate when a construction project is finished. We ought not to be too hard on ourselves if we find that we are training only a small fraction of that 100 percent, because I submit that many of them need a new job, not training.

COMMENT: Of the 5.1 million unemployed people between 1979 and 1984 who had been on a job for three consecutive years, 26 percent are still looking for work, 14 percent have left the work force altogether, 43 percent were out of work for at last twenty-seven weeks (which I see as a very long time), and 25 percent had periods of joblessness

MARVIN L. ESCH ET AL.

totaling a year or more. Those statistics seem neither encouraging nor productive.

MR. KOSTERS: Of course, I do not suggest that the displacement of workers or unemployment is desirable. But we should keep the problems of displaced workers in perspective and recognize that it is important to avoid reducing flexibility and attenuating incentives in our labor market, which has, on the whole, performed very well, especially compared with Europe, for example. As I have said, we should devote some resources to this problem, but we ought to be careful and realistic about how and how much.

MR. SAMUEL: I want to address one point that Mr. Kosters made earlier that most displaced workers got jobs that paid fairly well. I am not sure what "fairly well" is. Moreover, I do not consider our unemployment rate, now 7 percent or more if involuntary part-time workers and discouraged workers are included, very good. I don't think it is very good that the average displaced worker's job paid 15 percent less than the job he lost and that about a third took pay cuts of about 25 percent.

COMMENT: I think Mr. Samuel very effectively presented the AFL-CIO position, but an economist would suggest that one of the ways to make the United States more competitive is to bring its wage rates in line with other world economies. Some would ask, of course, if we wanted to reduce our wages to those of, say, Korea, to which some would reply that Korean wages should be brought up to ours.

MR. ESCH: Even as we move forward to become more competitive in an increasingly interdependent world, the human element is there. To the degree that we can develop affirmative public policies that do not intervene in the marketplace, that make us more competitive, and that still provide the basic human support systems necessary to fulfill the social contract, we have, indeed, fulfilled a significant public purpose.

Part Eight

Competitiveness:
A Major Campaign Issue in '88?

27

Is Competitiveness a Genuine Issue?

Norman Ornstein

This is obviously a time of political turmoil. It is a time of enormous flux in the political process—the first campaign since 1960 that is truly open, with no president running for reelection. The question of what will happen and how important issues will play out is particularly important given the lack of dominant issues in the campaign and on the campaign trail.

I am struck by the changing nature of American politics. In the span of barely more than a week we had the announcement of Texaco's bankruptcy, the announcement by Paul Simon of his candidacy for the presidency of the United States, and the announcement by Gary Hart of both. Of course, the flux does not occur just on the Democratic side of the aisle. It is an unusual presidential contest when one of the candidates on the Republican side, Pete DuPont, can run as the successor to Ronald Reagan because he would be the first genuine Teflon president, holding the trademark as he does on the material.

The questions we must address are these: Is competitiveness a genuine issue that grips the American people and that will provide a dominant theme for the candidates and the debate during the campaign in 1988? Will it therefore affect policy in the 100th Congress? Even more to the point, if it is a dominant theme in the campaign, will it carry forward into a top item on the agenda of the next president?

In some respects 1988 looks like 1960, not only because no incumbent is running and both parties have open contests, not only because we have a president leaving office who resembles in many respects the president who left office in 1960, Dwight Eisenhower, and not only because the economy and the openness of the political process look similar, but also because—perhaps as a result of all those things —there is no single, obvious, dominant issue engaging the public's attention. We do not have an economy that is going under for the third time. We do not have a deep foreign policy crisis that could provide the leitmotif for the campaign, just as we did not have a dominant issue in 1960. We had issues —the missile gap, Quemoy and Matsu—that became important themes in the campaign, valence issues. Nobody was for the missile gap; nobody was for giving up on Quemoy and Matsu.

Will competitiveness be the missile gap or the Quemoy and Matsu of 1988: an issue with some basis in reality but without the deep roots of more serious economic and foreign policy issues, one that will not divide the candidates in the normal fashion—nobody will be against competitiveness—but will, as those issues did, dominate some of the debate?

Whether this is a deeper issue than I am suggesting and whether it will be a dominant theme are questions we will discuss today , along with what we mean by competitiveness and how serious it is. Is it, in fact, simply a catch phrase, or is there something more to it?

28
A Democrat's View

Paul G. Kirk, Jr.

The fact that this conference is being held suggests that there is a problem in the area of competitiveness. We are not here to discuss how to sustain our trade surpluses or maintain our stable and diversified economic growth or our increasing productivity or even our rising standard of living. So the institute is to be lauded for addressing its attention to the issue. The question Will competitiveness be a major issue in 1988? suggests its own answer. On behalf of the Democrats, the answer is yes.

It is important to point out that competitiveness was an issue in many regions of the country and in the minds of the electorate in the Senate elections of 1986. It was an issue because there is a link, whether subconscious or conscious, with the economic concerns of families—their concerns about secure jobs and their standard of living —and their concerns about whether they will leave a richer and more rewarding life for their families than they inherited. That is what we believe as a country and as a party.

So the concept—not necessarily the word—does provide the kind of link with the political dynamics that will be taking place in 1988 as we talk about our economic future, the problems we need to address, and how families feel about their own economic future. It also relates to the desire of the American people to be number one or at least to excel in the global marketplace.

If this was a factor in 1986, it will be magnified in the national elections of 1988. The 1988 elections will not be decided on who devalued the dollar and by how much, or who supported which trade bill, who argued more vociferously for free trade, or who should be branded or acclaimed as a protectionist. Whether the word "competitiveness" is the focus of debate in 1988 is irrelevant. Some look at it as a meaningless buzzword, others as a political code word for protectionism. It is clear that to the electorate it will be a politically important issue.

The factors that will be looked at in the election of 1988, as in any election, will be performance and accountability on the record of the economy and how that is linked to people's feelings about the security of their future and where the nation is headed. Equally as important is which party or nominee will have the clearer and more compelling vision—the courage or the guts, if you will—to tell the American people that it is time we stopped borrowing and stealing from our future and instead begin to invest in it.

On the questions of the economic record, the party that came to office eight years ago on a promise of fiscal conservatism and on a promise to balance the budget by 1983 will be measured by their success in achieving these goals. We now have $220 billion in budget deficits, more than for all other presidents and administrations combined, from George Washington to Jimmy Carter, and the Republicans will be held accountable by the voters.

The trade deficit is $170 billion. We had a surplus in manufacturing goods in 1981, today we have a deficit of $108 billion. The national debt has been doubled. We have gone from the largest creditor to the largest debtor nation in the world. The American people see the arbitrageurs and the manipulators of money markets making millions, while millions of Americans who produce and work with their hands are either losing their jobs or heading into jobs that cannot pay as much.

That record of performance will be important. The Republicans are in the awkward situation of having to come to the American people and say, "Things have never been better, and we're the only party that can clean up this mess." They have a major problem of juxtaposition in how they reconcile what they say they are going to do with what they have done.

I will leave you with the notion that there is no quick fix. A combination of initiatives will be needed to move us back into a truly competitive relationship in the global marketplace and make people feel more secure about their future.

The most important element of the 1988 election from the Democratic party's point of view will be to have a nominee who will show the toughness of leadership and the clarity of vision, the pragmatism, the common sense, and the sheer courage to challenge the country to work together—public and private sectors, Democrats and Republicans, labor and management. The similarities to 1960 loom larger with every day.

In 1957, the launching of Sputnik was a challenge to our national security, if not a threat. Sputnik was a challenge to our economic strength and our entrepreneurial ingenuity and a challenge to the country to work together for a larger good. The Democratic candidates running are products of that generation. They remember 1957. They remember 1960. They remember also the past seven years. They remember that perhaps the most popular president went to the American people in 1984 and asked them: Are you better off than you were four years ago? They remember another popular Democrat in 1960 who had a different approach: Ask not what your country can do for you but what you can do for your country.

One is an appeal to personal self-interest, which is of interest in any election. The second is an appeal to patriotism, pride, national greatness, competitiveness, if you will, and a sense that if we're going to get through this, we'd better understand that we're going to have to work on it together.

What the Democrats will have, as they did in 1960, is not a set of promises but a set of challenges that go to the heart of these economic issues. My bet is that the country will respond, and that after two terms of a Republican administration the Democrats will carry the election and have the responsibility and mandate to rectify some of these problems.

29

A Republican's View

Edward J. Rollins

The term "competitiveness" has different meanings to different people, and for that reason it can be a double-edged sword. A few months ago some former colleagues of mine in the White House asked me if I could put together a group of labor supporters to go out and talk about competitiveness. I explained to them that when you talk to labor groups about competitiveness, they think you want them to work more hours for less pay. Unless you define the issue a little differently, you will not get much support in that sector. If you talk about competitiveness in education in terms of the need to make American students go to school fifty weeks a year, to compete with the Japanese, you can have a turned-off audience among both the teachers and the students. As the candidates raise the issue of competitiveness in 1988, then, they had better define very carefully what it means.

Trade, which is sometimes used as another word for competitiveness, can certainly be an issue in 1988. I have no idea what the dominant issue of 1988 will be, just as I am sure that neither Paul Kirk nor I can tell you who the nominees will be. I can probably pick the two teams that are going to play in the Super Bowl in January 1989 more easily than the candidates who are going to run against each other.

I agree that there are many similarities with 1960, and I believe the election will be very close—both in the percentage of the vote and in the electoral vote—regardless of who the nominees are. But the electorate is dramatically different.

What many people fail to realize is that the majority of voters in 1988 will be under forty-five. Competitiveness to them is: Are there going to be jobs in the future? Is there long-term stability? Have I gone to college and got a master's degree for nothing? What are the Japanese, who are not only buying buildings and hotels but are starting to buy industrial plants in the Midwest, going to do in the long term? It is all fun when we are making the Toyotas and the Hondas and the Sony television sets and filling the plants of Ohio and Tennessee and elsewhere, but what is going to happen in the long term?

It is not like the good old days, when someone could go into a steel plant or an auto plant in Detroit and look forward to a twenty- or twenty-five-year career. There is great uncertainty out there. The candidates who can respond to those issues will be the successful candidates.

There are some positive aspects to this issue. Candidates can be very future-oriented, can talk about the future shape of our economy. They have the opportunity to talk about pocketbook issues, even if the economy is sound or is starting to slide back a little.

Even though many of you in this room understand economics and trade deficits and what have you, most Americans don't. There are three economic indicators that mean something to most voters.

First, if unemployment starts to climb, they get very concerned. We found in 1982, when 10 percent of the American public was unemployed, that another 25 to 30 percent were worried about becoming unemployed. Each percentage point that the unemployment rate goes up creates more uncertainty.

Second, voters care about interest rates, which directly affect people buying homes. As someone who bought a home forty-five days ago, I am most appreciative of the fact that I bought it then rather than today. I saw on television that someone buying a $100,000 home with an $80,000 loan would be paying $320 a month more today than thirty days ago. I am very grateful that the one- or two-point change in the interest rates was not in effect then.

The third factor is certainly inflation. We have been in an inflationless period, but talk of trade sanctions and the like poses some significant dangers.

Those are the three factors the American public understands. They don't know what a trade deficit means. They don't know whether it is good or bad. They don't know if the Japanese or others coming in here and buying hotels and land and banks is good or bad.

Before I left the White House in 1985, I did a series of polls to find out where the American public stood on this issue. To my dismay Dick Wirthlin reported, "74 percent of the American public thinks we should put, or approves of putting, quotas or sanctions on the Japanese." I said, "That's very interesting, but I just can't believe that 75 percent of the American public wants to do anything. I don't think they quite understand the question."

So I suggested we put it a little differently the next month when we did our natiownide study: "If you want a sanction on the Japanese, does this mean that you are willing to pay 25 percent more for your Sony television set or 25 percent more for your Toyota or not to buy products from other countries?" The answer, of course, is no. As the candidates define this issue and debate it, a wide variety of reactions will come forth.

As Mr. Kirk said, the Democrats will point to this as a weak point in the presidential record. In 1984 they tried to make interest rates a weak point and to talk about the deficit and the need to raise taxes. Certainly, Mondale's victory in Minnesota was not an indication that the American public wanted an increase in taxes, and I don't think the Democratic candidates are going to advocate that in 1988. We would certainly like to see them do that, but I am sure they won't.

This issue will allow the candidates—particularly the Democrats in the primary process—in talking about competitive trade to do a little pandering. They can go to different groups and promise them diferent things. They can go to the farmers and make a particular speech. They can go to the Silicon Valley or the Research Triangle in Massachusetts and promise certain things, just as Gary Hart went into the steel areas of the country and said, "Elect me president, and I'll open the steel mill." I am very curious about what he intended to make in that steel mill.

There are some significant negatives to raising the issue. First, the issue may peak too soon. Democrats absolutely thought they had the issue of 1986. Even though it may have affected some races, I don't think it was only the trade issue that elected Democrats to the Senate in 1986.

In 1985 there was a special election in Texas. Republicans ran around the country saying, "We are going to win this." This was a test of realignment in the South, of whether the 1984 election meant anything. Nobody bothered to look at the fact that we had not elected a Republican in that district in a hundred years and probably won't for another hundred years. I have always been a great advocate of the belief that you can elect a bad candidate in a good district any day of the week. Skillful as we at this table may be at the campaign business, we cannot elect the best candidate in the world in a district that regularly votes 80 percent for the other party. The big issue of that campaign in Texas was that one of our candidates had Vote-America hats that were made in Taiwan. So Tony Coelho and others thought they had the issue: trade.

It was a little too soon. It is very worthwhile for the candidates in 1988 to debate trade policy and try to educate the American public. It is one of the most significant problems that we as Americans are going to face, and it has no simple solutions.

124

I don't think anybody in this room is going to predict that we will be in the depths of recession in 1988. If any of you are, you are the same ones who were predicting a recession in 1984, 1985, and 1986. I don't think anybody knows where we are going to be. Certainly, there is still some growth, and there are still some factors we are not happy with.

There are a lot of uncertainties out there today, and Americans have many concerns. I just hope we will not get into pandering in this campaign but that we will get into educating the public.

We also have to examine the pocketbook issues. What are the effects of sanctions and quotas and the various entities being debated in the Congress and in the administration? Are American consumers in the habit of buying Sony television sets and Walkmans and what have you? Are they willing to give them up? Are they willing to pay higher prices? Is the tariff that the administration is about to put on 1.5 percent of Japanese imports a penalty on the Japanese, or is it a penalty on American consumers?

That is the debate that is going to rage. Some of the Republicans who will be talking about fair trade, as opposed to just free trade, will have some interesting solutions. The American public might be more satisfied if we decided to have every Toyota or Nissan that landed on the docks of San Francisco and Long Beach and Oakland inspected to make sure it met all the National Traffic Safety Agency (NTSA) requirements. If the inspectors got through fifty a day, that is how many could be sold. That could still be fair trade because that is exactly what happens to many of our products overseas. That may have more appeal to the American public than a 25 or 50 percent quota that would raise the prices they have to pay and would have some significant backlash.

It is going to be a fascinating election cycle. Those of us who are in this business and participants in the process certainly feel handicapped because we don't know the answers to who is going to do what, who is going to say what. If any of you have a magic solution or a magic message, my candidate would certainly want to run with it.

We are in a unique political climate. The voters are turned off, apathetic, disillusioned. It becomes imperative for the candidates to articulate effectively what they are going to stand for and what the leadership of this country is going to stand for in the 1990s and the year 2000.

I don't think Mr. Kirk wants his candidates to talk about more tax-and-spend programs. I'm sure that our candidates will not be successful if they say only, "Give us eight more years of the Reagan administration." The debate is going to be very heated. Both parties are going to redefine themselves. The party that hits the pulse beat of the American public may be the party that leads us into the future.

The tasks are extremely difficult. I don't envy the candidate who walks into the Oval Office on January 20, 1989, because the problems facing the country are significant. It is imperative that we work closely together regardless of whether we have a Democratic or a Republican president, a Democratic or a Republican Congress. Unless we put some of our partisanship aside after the election and work collectively with common sense, we will have significant long-term problems.

30

What the Polls Tell Us

Karlyn H. Keene

Today I would like to talk about the ambiguities that we see in public opinion data and how I think they will play into the larger issue of competitiveness.

Ed Rollins is absolutely correct. When the pollsters ask about protecting American jobs by imposing import restrictions, solid majorities of Americans—usually 50 to 65 percent—support those restrictions. But what is particularly interesting about that opinion is that it has not evolved over a long period.

When the Roper organization first asked about import restrictions to protect jobs, about 65 percent of Americans favored such restrictions. When he posed the question again last year, fifteen years later, the same majority approved. If the question suggests that Americans might be paying more for their Sony televisions or their Walkmans, that percentage diminishes, but it is still strong.

That simple reading of public opinion would suggest that someone like Dick Gephardt has struck political gold with the legislation he is pushing on Capitol Hill. But the public opinion picture is rarely simple, and it is filled with ambiguity. Public opinion is equally strong on a range of other trade-related issues but comes down on a very different side.

When the Roper organization recently asked Americans about foreign competition and its effect on American manufacturers, equally strong majorities said that foreign competition makes American manufacturers more competitive and enables them to make products at a lower cost for all consumers. Over 80 percent of Americans agreed in a recent Harris Poll that to compete we must produce better products more efficiently rather than depend on artificial trade barriers. An NBC News–*Wall Street Journal* poll last month found solid majorities of Americans saying that we do not work as hard as some of our competitors and that our companies are not as efficient. And in a

Yankelovich survey of public attitudes toward Japan, 68 percent of Americans surveyed said that the Japanese are successful because they produce better products at better prices. Only a quarter said that the reason was unfair trade practices. Americans believe, according to Yankelovich, that Japan is more successful and that its success has been earned.

This set of questions shows that Americans believe that free trade is the best way to organize our economy. Over and over again that theme permeates the surveys on public opinion.

Thus we have a picture of remarkably stable, though contradictory, attitudes in public opinion over a very long period. On the one hand, Americans support protection; on the other hand, they put the blame right here in the United States and suggest that we simply are not competing effectively enough.

A more important question is: What is really driving the issue to the front pages of our newspapers today? What is all the fuss about if public opinion hasn't changed in fifteen years? I would like to suggest four possible explanations—again, through the prism of survey data.

The first is an obvious one that all the speakers have been talking about—objective conditions. Americans clearly recognize that we are now a global economy. As Ed Rollins and Paul Kirk said, they cannot tell you much about what that means, but they clearly realize that we are now interdependent in a way that we have never been before.

The Roper organization posed a wonderful question last month. They asked Americans about twelve products, including the Ford Taurus, Dodge Aries, GE microwaves, and RCA videocassette recorders. They asked whether these products were made entirely in the United States, only partly in the United States, or for the most part abroad.

Confusion reigned. In no single instance were Americans able to tell the pollsters where the product was made or even if it was made mainly in the United States.

Thus Americans are looking at these issues with a great deal of confusion and ambiguity in their minds. They are looking for leadership. The objective indicators are driving their concerns.

A second reason that both the speakers have touched on is the public's generalized concern and uneasiness about the state of the American economy. We are in the fifth year of an economic expansion, Americans are savoring an economic climate that they have not experienced for quite a long time. Conditions are far different from the late 1970s and early 1980s, when opinion polls showed about 65 percent of Americans were concerned about inflation, or 1981 and

1982, when about 65 percent were saying that the unemployment rate was their major concern.

For some time they have had a president who has had almost perfect pitch with their concerns, and he has made them optimistic about the future. Now they are not so sure about him, and that uneasiness is driving their concerns, too.

The third reason, which is perhaps the most important, has to do not so much with public opinion as with elite opinion. We have seen a remarkable transformation of elite attitudes in the past two decades. The elite consensus on free trade has weakened considerably. While public opinion has remained stable, the elite consensus has begun to break down. The virtually monolithic view that free trade is the best way to organize the economy has been under assault as individual companies have sought relief or protection, however you prefer to characterize it. This has changed the policy climate dramatically.

A fourth reason is that politics, like nature, abhors a vacuum. This is a virtually issueless time. Public opinion polls find no issue that bothers more than 15 to 20 percent of Americans. We haven't seen a period like that in a very long time.

Paul Kirk suggested that the trade or competitiveness issue garnered the Democrats some votes in a few key races in the 1986 elections. In the exit polls by CBS and the *New York Times* in fifteen key states, they asked voters what was the most important issue affecting their vote. Trade was one of the categories offered, one of the boxes they could check. Only 10 percent or less of Americans in thirteen of those fifteen states said that trade had been the most important issue to them. Only in North Carolina and Pennsylvania did more than 10 percent of Americans say the issue had mattered most to them. In Pennsylvania it was 11 percent, and in North Carolina it was 15.

We are not seeing many issues in the double digits. Thus any issue, particularly an issue like competitiveness, can take center stage. When there are no overriding issues in American politics, secondary ones can have their day in the sun, and the sun is certainly shining on competitiveness.

As I look ahead to the 1988 election, I believe competitiveness is unlikely to generate much electoral heat. Perhaps it will generate more light.

When an issue is as subject to varied interpretation as competitiveness, it really ceases to be an issue in American politics. Any savvy politician can embrace it; that is what has happened on Capitol Hill. The definitions vary, but Republicans are endorsing it, Democrats are endorsing it, conservatives are endorsing it, and liberals are endorsing it.

I'm not sure whether the issue will be the missile gap of 1988. But I think we will be likely to hear as much about competitiveness in 1988 as we heard about industrial policy, the balanced budget amendment, the nuclear freeze, and a whole range of issues that enjoyed their day in the sun but faded very quickly.

31

The Meaning of Competitiveness

Karlyn H. Keene, Paul G. Kirk, Jr., Norman Ornstein,
Edward J. Rollins, and John H. Makin

MR. ORNSTEIN: Ed Rollins started our focus on public opinion, hitting very accurately what Americans see and understand and what moves them in the economic vocabulary. Clearly, "trade deficit" is not one of those terms.

Using the word "competitiveness" is a way of taking an issue that does not resound for the public and making it resound. We want to be competitive in everything. We are sports fans. We watch horse races and political contests. The notion of appealing to patriotism by suggesting that it's us against them does get juices flowing.

We can take an issue of that sort and make it all things to all people. We can talk about competitiveness in education and not necessarily make it the onerous burden for students or teachers of working longer. Instead Democrats can talk about increasing federal involvement in education and frame it in terms of competitiveness. In the same way, by framing it in terms of competitiveness, Republicans can talk about unleashing industry without having to take the flak of being for big business. To whatever degree it can be cloaked as a patriotic issue that nobody can be against, everybody can gain some benefits from it.

MR. KIRK: I would reinforce that point. I think the trade issue within the context of "competitiveness" is too narrow. But the spirit of the country and national pride can be pointed to and tapped.

The other point is not just the trade deficit but the continuous and growing debt on all fronts and the fact that families are amassing great personal debt. All of that leads to an erosion of confidence in the future.

There is a deep-seated concern about it and it will get deeper unless we are prepared to address it. The other thing that I hope people recognized as we were talking is that both Ed Rollins and I agree that whatever happens in this election, both political parties and their leaders and their people must work together to get through this.

Americans want to be challenged. They want to see competition. Everybody knows that for an athlete or a team to be great takes training and sacrifice. A combination of these things is going to flow into the dialogue of the 1988 campaign.

Ms. KEENE: I see the trade issue as a problem, in some ways, for Democrats. This is something we haven't touched on yet, and it relates to the question about optimism. One problem the Democrats have had in the past several elections is that they have been perceived as the party of doom and gloom. The Republicans have used optimism. Reagan, in particular, has seized it and taken it away from the Democrats.

One concern about the way Gephardt, in particular, is using the trade issue is that it begins to take on a slightly defeatist attitude—the perception that Americans cannot compete. Right now the Democrats are handling it very successfully, but the issue has that potential. It is something we have to be concerned about, because optimism is extremely important. But if it becomes defeatism—America cannot win—it can turn into a real negative for the Democrats. It has to be handled very carefully.

MR. ROLLINS: I agree. There has been an optimistic belief in the great American comeback and morning in America and so forth. People in this country are optimistic; but because we have seen a series of presidents fail, there is continued disillusionment.

My central point is that the problems will not be solved by one nominee or one president. People have to believe that unless they are part of the team and part of the action, we are not going to get through this. The campaign is going to be more a challenge and a stirring of those emotions than a pandering and playing to them.

MR. ORNSTEIN: It seems to me that this issue gets raised for another reason; that is, it taps into the fundamental American value of fairness. Nothing moves us more than the notion of fairness, either domestically or in a broader context. Gephardt raises the issue much more in terms of fairness than in terms of "we've got to tighten our belts." It is much more that we are playing by one set of rules and all these other people are playing by another, and it's unfair and we're not going to take it anymore. If that has a broader appeal, it is a theme that can win votes.

I also see a danger in all of this. If we frame things in terms of us against them and all those countries being unfair, even though they are our allies in many other areas, don't we create complications for ourselves and the world, where we already see our relations with our allies frayed on many other fronts?

MR. ROLLINS: Those are excellent points. I just want to comment as one of the architects of "morning again in America." We didn't say because it was morning again you didn't have to get up and go to work. There is always a tendency to forget that.

We are the ultimate consumer nation in the world. We buy more junk and more products than any other country. If we ever got a little bit of American pride once again, particularly among many of the young people, we might make a deliberate decision that one out of five shirts we were going to buy was going to be made in the United States and so on. The Japanese people are trained from birth to buy their own. In this country we have gotten away from that. It could be very productive if our candidates talked about having a little pride in the United States and buying some American products.

MR. MAKIN: The world has changed so much that you really cannot be sure whether you are buying an American product. For example, when you buy an IBM-PC, about 80 percent of its value is in assorted components. Many automobiles manufactured by Chrysler, Ford, and others are heavily composed of foreign components.

Of course, this is one of the reasons the trade statistics are misleading. A lot of American sales are made in Japan. In some ways the American companies are doing very well. The companies that are doing well happen to be innovative and not contributing to our numbers. It is really a question of the way the world has become highly integrated. I agree with Karlyn Keene that the competitiveness issue will be a difficult one to hang on to the campaign, because of the tenuous link between nations and national pride and a particular product.

COMMENT: It is not simply a question of how tough we can be on others, although there may be instances where we should be and have to be. The more important question about this issue and the situation the country is in is how serious we are going to be about ourselves and what we have to do to get ourselves on a larger growth track, in a more expansive economy, and invest in our own future. That is one of the things serious-minded candidates for the leadership of this country will have to talk about.

QUESTION: Do you think he'd get away with it, or wouldn't we just call him a doom-and-gloom Democrat?

MR. KIRK: No, because this country has to be challenged about these issues. We cannot just wring our hands or state how bad the record of the Republicans might be. Speaking as a Democrat, I think people want to know not what is worse about the other guy, but what we are going to do about it.

That goes back to what Karlyn Keene and Ed Rollins have both said about the polling data. People in this country are continually disillusioned, and they are tired of being conned. Candidates cannot succeed with promises and pandering. They need common-sense talk: here's where it is, it relates to your future and your family.

COMMENT: What has been curious about this discussion is that everyone says the issues are all much the same—trade, education, foreign competition. Competitiveness is a fair enough umbrella to put all those issues under. Yet at the same time it seems that everyone is backing away from using "competitiveness." The terms "excellence" and "prosperity" do not really capture the idea as closely. Is it a question of semantics, or is it that as far as the political issue goes, we are trying to get too much at once?

COMMENT: The great difficulty is that the issue means different things to different people and different audiences. One of the difficulties the candidates of both parties are going to have is that there are some very divergent views. Certainly some Democrats think protectionism is healthy. Many think it is an absolute disaster. Many Republicans would love to jump on the protectionist bandwagon because of parochial interest in their home state but also fear a nationwide backlash against it. The uncertainty about where we go and what our solutions are is causing a lack of definiteness about how the candidates are going to run.

MR. KIRK: I'd say it is a matter of semantics. People care about families, about individuals, about the country at large, about leaving a better situation than they found. Perhaps they are working harder than their parents did, not making ends meet, not leaving what they want for their kids. What does all that mean? A lot of this is going to revolve about whether we are going to have a brighter future: whether competitiveness is the right word seems to me not relevant. We need to tap into those values that bring the country together and put it on a positive track.

Ms. Keene: I agree with what has been said, but I have a bit of a problem with the word. That is because I think American politics is about opposing ideas, although we want to unite and move the country ahead. This word, because it has been embraced by nearly every element of the political spectrum, will be difficult to use to differentiate the candidates as we move ahead to 1988.

Certainly, the things under the umbrella will differentiate the candidates, and those are the things that will turn out to be important. There are specific policy differences between a Dick Gephardt and a Gary Hart on trade, between the Republicans and the Democrats, but the word itself is too broad to be meaningful in a political context. It may be a great word for an acceptance speech.

Glossary of International Trade Terms

Adjustment Assistance. Financial, training, and reemployment technical assistance to workers and technical assistance to firms and industries to help them cope with adjustment difficulties arising from increased import competition. The objective of the assistance is usually to help an industry to become more competitive in the same line of production or to move into other economic activities.

Agency for International Development (AID). The unit within the U.S. government responsible for the administration of U.S. bilateral development assistance programs. AID also participates actively in the development of other U.S. policies and programs related to third world economic development.

Article I, section 8 of the Constitution. The principal source of the legislative branch's authority in international trade matters. It specifically empowers Congress to "lay and collect Taxes, Duties, Imports and Excises" and to "regulate commerce with foreign Nations."

Balance of Payments. A tabulation of a country's credit and debit transactions with other countries and international institutions.

Balance of Trade. A component of the balance of payments or the surplus or deficit that results from comparing a country's expenditures on merchandise imports and receipts derived from its merchandise exports.

Beggar-Thy-Neighbor Policy. A course of action through which a country tries to reduce unemployment and increase domestic output through competitive devaluation or by raising tariffs and instituting nontariff barriers that impede imports.

This glossary of international trade terms was adapted from material prepared by the Department of Commerce and the U.S. Information Agency.

Comparative Advantage. A central concept in international trade theory which holds that a country or region should specialize in the production and export of those goods and services that it can produce relatively more efficiently than other goods and services, and import those goods and services in which it has a comparative disadvantage.

Council for Mutual Economic Assistance (COMECON or CMEA). An intergovernmental organization established in 1949 to coordinate the economies of member states and now consisting of the Soviet Union, Bulgaria, Czechoslovakia, the German Democratic Republic (East Germany), Hungary, Mongolia, Poland, Romania, Cuba, and Vietnam.

Current Account. That portion of a country's balance of payments that records current (as opposed to capital) transactions, including visible trade (exports and imports), invisible trade (income and expenditures for services), profits earned from foreign operations, interest, and transfer payments.

Dumping. Under U.S. law, the sale of an imported commodity in the United States at "less than fair value," usually considered to be a price lower than that at which it is sold within the exporting country or to third countries.

Escape Clause. A provision in a bilateral or multilateral commercial agreement permitting a signatory nation to suspend tariff or other concessions when imports threaten serious harm to the producers of competitive domestic goods.

European Community (EC). A popular term for the European Communities that resulted from the 1967 "Treaty of Fusion" that merged the secretariat (the Commission) and the intergovernmental executive body (the Council) of the older European Economic Community (EEC) with those of the European Coal and Steel Community (ECSC) and the European Atomic Energy Community (EURATOM), which was established to develop nuclear fuel and power for civilian purposes. The EEC first came into operation on Jan. 1, 1958, based on the Treaty of Rome, with six participating member states (France, Italy, the Federal Republic of Germany, Belgium, the Netherlands, and Luxembourg). From the beginning, a principal objective of the Community was the establishment of a customs union, other forms of economic integration, and political cooperation among member countries. The Treaty of Rome provided for the gradual elimination of customs duties and other internal trade barriers, the establishment of a common external tariff, and guarantees of free movement of labor and capital within the Community. The United Kingdom, Denmark, and Ireland joined the Community in 1973, Greece in 1981, and Spain and Portugal in 1986. Community headquarters are in Brussels.

Exchange Rate. The price (or rate) at which one currency is exchanged for another currency, for gold, or for Special Drawing Rights (SDRs).

Export Quotas. Specific restrictions or ceilings imposed by an exporting country on the value or volume of certain imports, designed to protect domestic producers and consumers from temporary shortages of the goods affected or to bolster their prices in world markets.

Export Restraints. Quantitative restrictions imposed by exporting countries to limit exports to specified foreign markets, usually pursuant to a formal or informal agreement concluded at the request of the importing countries.

Export Subsidies. Government payments or other financially quantifiable benefits provided to domestic producers or exporters contingent on the export of their goods or services.

Free Trade. A theoretical concept that assumes international trade unhampered by government measures such as tariffs or nontariff barriers. The objective of trade liberalization is to achieve "freer trade" rather than "free trade," it being generally recognized among trade policy officials that some restrictions on trade are likely to remain in effect for the foreseeable future.

Free Trade Area. A group of two or more countries that have eliminated tariff and most nontariff barriers affecting trade among themselves, while each participating country applies its own independent schedule of tariffs to imports from countries that are not members.

General Agreement on Tariffs and Trade (GATT). A multilateral trade agreement aimed at expanding international trade as a means of raising world welfare. GATT rules reduce uncertainty in connection with commercial transactions across national borders. Ninety-two countries accounting for approximately 80 percent of world trade are Contracting Parties to GATT, and some thirty additional countries associated with it benefit from the application of its provisions to their trade. The designation "GATT" also refers to the organization headquartered at Geneva through which the General Agreement is enforced. This organization provides a framework within which international negotiations—known as "Rounds"—are conducted to lower tariffs and other barriers to trade, and a consultative mechanism that may be invoked by governments seeking to protect their trade interests.

Generalized System of Preferences (GSP). The GSP reflects a concept developed within UNCTAD to encourage the expansion of manufactured and semimanufactured exports from developing countries by making goods more competitive in developed country markets through tariff preferences.

Gephardt Amendment. A provision of the House omnibus trade bill H.R. 3. It requires the president to enter into negotiations or otherwise take action to reduce trade deficits with countries that register "excessive" trade surpluses with the United States and that employ unfair trading practices. If negotiations fail, the amendment requires the president to impose quotas or other measures sufficient to reduce the deficit by 10 percent annually for five years. The president could waive imposition of quotas if it were determined that they would harm the U.S. economy or that the offending country had balance-of-payments difficulties and could not reduce its surplus with the United States without experiencing significant economic hardship.

H.R. 3. The omnibus trade bill introduced to the House of Representatives, January 6, 1987. It passed the House with amendments on April 30, 1987, and was referred to the Senate.

Import Substitution. An attempt by a country to reduce imports (and hence foreign exchange expenditures) by encouraging the development of domestic industries.

Industrial Policy. Encompasses traditional government policies intended to provide a favorable economic climate for the development of industry in general or specific industrial sectors. Instruments of industrial policy may include tax incentives to promote investments or exports, direct or indirect subsidies, special financing arrangements, protection against foreign competition, worker training programs, regional development programs, assistance for research and development, and measures to help small business firms.

Most-Favored-Nation Treatment (MFN). The policy of nondiscrimination in trade policy that provides to all trading partners the same customs and tariff treatment given to the so-called "most-favored nation." This fundamental principle was a feature of U.S. trade policy as early as 1778. Since 1923 the United States has incorporated an "unconditional" most-favored-nation clause in its trade agreements, binding the contracting governments to confer upon each other all the most favorable trade concessions that either may grant to any other country subsequent to the signing of the agreement. The United States now applies this provision to its trade with all of its trading partners except for those specifically excluded by law.

Multi-Fiber Arrangement Regarding International Trade in Textiles (MFA). An international compact under GATT that allows an importing signatory country to apply quantitative restrictions on textiles imports when it considers them necessary to prevent market disruption.

Multilateral Trade Negotiations (MTN). Seven Rounds of multilateral trade negotiations have been held under the auspices of GATT since 1947. Each Round represented a discrete and lengthy series of interacting bargaining sessions among the participating Contracting Parties in search of mutually beneficial agreements looking toward the reduction of barriers to world trade.

Newly Industrializing Countries (NICs). Relatively advanced developing countries whose industrial production and exports have grown rapidly in recent years. Examples include Brazil, Hong Kong, Korea, Mexico, Singapore, and Taiwan.

Non-Tariff Barriers (NTBs). Government measures other than tariffs that restrict imports. Such measures have become relatively more conspicuous impediments to trade as tariffs have been reduced during the period since World War II.

Organization for Economic Cooperation and Development (OECD). An organization based in Paris with a membership of the twenty-four developed countries. Their basic aims are to achieve the highest sustainable economic growth and employment while maintaining financial stability: and to contribute to sound economic expansion worldwide and to the expansion of world trade on a multilateral, nondiscriminatory basis. The OECD succeeded the Organization for European Economic Corporation (OEEC) in 1961, after the post–World War II economic reconstruction of Europe had been largely accomplished.

Protectionism. The deliberate use or encouragement of restrictions on imports to enable relatively inefficient domestic producers to compete successfully with foreign producers.

Reciprocity. The practice by which governments extend similar concessions to each other, as when one government lowers its tariffs or other barriers impeding its imports in exchange for equivalent concessions from a trading partner on barriers affecting its exports (a "balance of concessions").

Retaliation. Action taken by a country to restrain its imports from a country that has increased a tariff or imposed other measures that adversely affect its exports in a manner inconsistent with GATT.

Round of Trade Negotiations. A cycle of multilateral trade negotiations under the aegis of GATT, culminating in simultaneous trade agreements among participating countries to reduce tariff and nontariff barriers to trade. Seven Rounds have been completed thus far: Geneva, 1947–1948; Annecy, France, 1949; Torquay, England, 1950–1951; Geneva, 1956; Geneva, 1960–1962 (the Dillon Round); 1963–1967 (the Kennedy Round); and Geneva, 1973–1979 (the Tokyo Round).

Section 201 (of the Trade Act of 1974). Sometimes referred to as the "escape clause" law because it sets forth U.S. procedures that can lead to the invoking of the escape clause in Article XIX of the General Agreement on Tariffs and Trade. This provision of U.S. law authorizes domestic industries seriously injured by increased imports to petition the U.S. International Trade Commission (ITC) for relief in the form of higher tariffs, quotas, or adjustment assistance. If the ITC finds substantial injury due to imports, it can recommend that the president impose relief. This statute deals with fairly traded imports and is designed to give U.S. companies time to adjust to import competition.

Section 301 (of the Trade Act of 1974). Provision of U.S. law that enables the president to withdraw concessions or restrict imports from countries that discriminate against U.S. exports, subsidize their own exports to the United States, or engage in other unjustifiable or unreasonable practices that burden or discriminate against U.S. trade.

Services. Economic activities—such as transportation, banking, insurance, tourism, space launching telecommunications, advertising, entertainment, data processing, consulting, and the licensing of intellectual property—that are usually of an intangible character and often consumed as they are produced.

Smoot-Hawley Tariff Act of 1930. U.S. protectionist legislation that raised tariff rates on most articles imported by the United States, triggering comparable tariff increases by U.S. trading partners. The Tariff Act of 1930 is also known as the Smoot-Hawley Tariff.

Subsidy. An economic benefit granted by a government to producers of goods, often to strengthen their competitive position. The subsidy may be direct (a cash grant) or indirect (low-interest export credits guaranteed by a government agency, for example).

Tariff. A duty (or tax) levied upon goods transported from one customs area to another. Tariffs raise the prices of imported goods, thus making them less competitive within the market of the importing country. After seven Rounds of GATT trade negotiations that focused heavily on tariff reductions, tariffs are less important measures of protection than they used to be. The term "tariff" often refers to a comprehensive list or "schedule" of merchandise with the rate of duty to be paid to the government for importing products listed.

Transfer of Technology. The movement of modern or scientific methods of production or distribution from one enterprise, institution, or country to another, as through foreign investment, international trade licensing of patent rights, technical assistance, or training.

U.S. International Trade Commission (USITC). Formerly the U.S. Tariff Commission, which was created in 1916 by an Act of Congress. Its mandate was broadened and its name changed by the Trade Act of 1974. It is an independent fact-finding agency of the U.S. government that studies the effects of tariffs and other restraints to trade on the U.S. economy. It conducts public hearings to assist in determining whether particular U.S. industries are injured or threatened with injury by dumping, export subsidies in other countries, or rapidly rising imports. It also studies the probable economic impact on specific U.S. industries of proposed reductions in U.S. tariffs and nontariff barriers to imports. Its six members are appointed by the president with the advice and consent of the U.S. Senate for nine-year terms.

United States Trade Representative (USTR). A cabinet-level official with the rank of ambassador who is the principal adviser to the U.S. president on international trade policy. The U.S. trade representative is concerned with the expansion of U.S. exports, U.S. participation in GATT, commodity issues, East-West and North-South trade, and direct investment related to trade. As chairman of the U.S. Trade Policy Committee, he is also the primary official responsible for U.S. participation in all international trade negotiations. Prior to the Trade Agreements Act of 1979, which created the Office of the U.S. Trade Representative, the comparable official was known as the President's Special Representative for Trade Negotiations (STR), a position first established by the Trade Expansion Act of 1962.

Voluntary Restraint Agreements (VRAs). Informal arrangements through which exporters voluntarily restrain certain exports, usually through export quotas, to avoid economic dislocation in an importing country, and to avert the possible imposition of mandatory import restrictions. Such arrangements do not normally entail "compensation" for the exporting country.

World Bank. The International Bank for Reconstruction and Development (IBRD), commonly referred to as the World Bank, is an intergovernmental financial institution located in Washington, D.C. Its objectives are to help raise productivity and incomes and reduce poverty in developing countries. It was established in December 1945 on the basis of a plan developed at the Bretton Woods Conference of 1944. The bank loans financial resources to credit worthy developing countries. It raises most of its funds by selling bonds in the world's major capital markets.